P9-DTN-107

CREATIVE MUSEUM METHODS
AND
EDUCATIONAL TECHNIQUES

CREATIVE MUSEUM METHODS
AND
EDUCATIONAL TECHNIQUES

By

JEANETTE HAUCK BOOTH

Coordinator of School Programs
The Children's Museum
Indianapolis, Indiana

GERALD H. KROCKOVER

Professor of Education and Geosciences
Purdue University
West Lafayette, Indiana

and

PAULA R. WOODS

Curator of Education
Tippecanoe County Historical Association
Lafayette, Indiana

CHARLES C THOMAS • PUBLISHER
Springfield • Illinois • U.S.A.

Published and Distributed Throughout the World by

CHARLES C THOMAS • PUBLISHER
2600 South First Street
Springfield, Illinois, 62717, U.S.A.

© *1982 by* CHARLES C THOMAS • PUBLISHER

ISBN 0-398-04694-8

Library of Congress Catalog Card Number: 82-3353

*With THOMAS BOOKS careful attention is given to all details of
manufacturing and design. It is the Publisher's desire to present books that are
satisfactory as to their physical qualities and artistic possibilities and
appropriate for their particular use. THOMAS BOOKS will be true to those
laws of quality that assure a good name and good will.*

Printed in the United States of America
I-RX-1

Library of Congress Cataloging in Publication Data

Booth, Jeanette Hauck.
Creative museum methods and educational techniques.

Bibliography: p.
Includes index.
1. Museums — Educational aspects. I. Krockover, Gerald H. II. Woods, Paula R.
III. Title.

AM7.B65   069.1'5   82-3353
ISBN 0-398-04694-8   AACR2

A CHILD is a person who is going to carry on what you have started. He is going to sit where you are sitting, and when you are gone, attend to those things which you think are important. You may adopt all the policies you please, but how they are carried out depends on him. He will assume control of your cities, states, and nations. He is going to move in and take over your churches, schools, universities, and corporations. All your books are going to be judged, praised or condemned by him. The fate of humanity is in his hands.

Abraham Lincoln

PREFACE

ACCORDING to a survey conducted by the National Center for Educational Statistics (NCES), the nation's museums are spending more on educational services and activities than ever before. More than two-thirds of the 4,408 museums surveyed in 1980 were increasing their education programs, and furthermore, they ranked education programs second only to their exhibits. Almost nine out of every ten museums offer tours for elementary school students, and three-fourths offer special tours for high school students. More than two-thirds have special programs earmarked for specific audiences, such as adults, senior citizens, preschoolers, minorities, gifted and talented children, and the disabled visitor.

In spite of all of this educational activity, many museums utilize museum personnel with little or no background in either education or museums. Most museum personnel must search for resources that will help them organize a docent training program. Docents, once selected, need a reference that can assist them in defining their role in a museum and what they should be expected to do, since the primary means that museums respond to their clientele is through tours, mainly guided tours.

This book can serve as a sourcebook for docent training programs, either as the entire general training guide or as an additional reference. It can be used by both the docent trainer and by individual docents. It attempts to incorporate into one reference source information about museum education. Most of the material is a direct result of the authors' experience in docent education programs and includes topics basic to all docent education programs in order to provide a firm foundation for the guided tour. This book also provides the means for museums to continue their emphasis upon the development of professional museum education programs. As a result, this book can be used as a source of ideas for specific docent education programs, as a basis for new programs and the refinement of old programs, as a docent education program guide and as an individual docent guide. This book should also serve to expand one's horizon, to introduce new docent education methods and techniques, and to improve docent education programs.

Chapter 1, Museums — Informal Versus Formal Education, explores the role of the docent in museums, the docent as part of the museum, and how to work with a variety of museum visitors. Chapter 2, Inquiry Educational Methods, presents ideas and suggestions for docent training programs and workshops. Techniques that are presented include the following: questioning levels, posing questions, wait time, involving visitors, organizing the flow of the guided visit, and introducing a visit. Chapter 3, Educational Programs, explores the variety of methods that can be used to meet the needs of the museum visitor: dynamic exhibits, educational kits, games, role playing, searches, problem solving activities, simulation activities, tactile experiences, guided visit themes, and the use of travelling exhibits. Chapter 4, Working With People, introduces creative methods and techniques that docents can utilize with museum visitors, such as group dynamics, enhancing interpersonal relationships, enhancing discussion and disagreement, utilizing Piagetian learning levels, analyzing the capabilities, skills, and interests of the group, utilizing scheduling, and procedures for working with a group. Chapter 5, Working With Special Groups, responds to the need for training docents to meet the special concerns of handicapped, gifted, slow learning, primary, nursery school, nonschool, nonpublic school, teenage, and special interest visitors. Chapter 6, Evaluating Museum Programs, provides the methods and techniques for evaluating the docent and tours. Also included are sample evaluation materials and a rationale for setting up an evaluation scheme. A comprehensive bibliography is also included for those docents who wish to pursue particular subjects in greater depth, to affiliate with a professional museum organization, or to utilize audiovisual materials.

We hope that *Creative Museum Methods and Educational Techniques* will assist you in developing yourself, your docents, and your guided tours to their fullest. For only then can the museum begin to fulfill its role as our cultural educator of the past, present, and future.

Jeanette Hauck Booth
Gerald H. Krockover
Paula R. Woods

ACKNOWLEDGMENTS

W E would like to thank M. Bernadette Malady and Kathy Shelton for their assistance in the preparation of this manuscript.

CONTENTS

CREATIVE MUSEUM METHODS
AND
EDUCATIONAL TECHNIQUES

Chapter 1
MUSEUMS: INFORMAL VERSUS FORMAL EDUCATION

Education makes us what we are.
C. A. Helvetius, 1715 — 1771

I N the 1970s, museums in the United States were confronted
with two major issues that were to greatly alter their direction: accreditation and accountability. Accreditation is the process by which an organization grants official recognition to an institution that has conformed to a set of preestablished minimum
qualifications stipulated by the organization itself. By undergoing
the accrediting process an institution accomplished the following:
— Certification
— Self-improvement
— Eligibility for public funding
— Increased public status
Museum accreditation resulted from the efforts of the American Association of Museums (AAM), the professional organization of United States museums, to develop a definitive statement
describing a museum and to establish a set of common standards
for evaluating a museum's professional competence since before
the accreditation program, museum performance standards dif-
fered greatly. Museum professionals felt a need to provide consistent, clearly stated guidelines, professional standards by which a
museum could be judged, and to initiate the process of self-
evaluation for the museum community. Accreditation was also
viewed as a way of providing private and governmental agencies

some decision-making criteria for evaluating requests by museums for contributions, grants, and contracts.

In 1968, an AAM committee was formed to study the problem of accreditation and to prepare a report that would aid in establishing minimal standards for the museum profession. When the accreditation committee presented its final report to the AAM council in 1970, its recommendations were formally accepted by the association. For the purposes of accreditation the AAM defines a museum as "an organized and permanent non-profit organization, essentially educational or aesthetic in purpose, with professional staff, which owns and utilizes tangible objects, cares for them, and exhibits them to the public on a regular schedule."[1] Any institution meeting this definition is viewed as a museum by the commission and can be considered for accreditation. On the other hand, an institution that does not meet this definition is ineligible for accreditation consideration.

In 1975, the commission broadened the definition of a museum to embody institutions that do not necessarily own and utilize tangible objects of intrinsic value so that they might be considered for accreditation. Such institutions must adhere to all the other elements of the fundamental museum definition and must constitute a separate category consisting of other like institutions. Out of this broadened definition evolved three distinct types of institutions: planetariums, science and technology centers, and art centers. The accreditation process forced museums to scrutinize themselves by predetermined evaluative criteria and to validate their professional status by conforming to the AAM standards of professionalism.

The AAM definition of a museum committed the museum community to educating the public, and American museums soon found themselves confronted with the issues of social relevancy and accountability. In the United States, there was a movement to hold institutions accountable for the achievement of their stated goals and objectives. The urban minorities decried the museum's lack of relevancy to their lives and demanded that museums be held responsible for educating not only its middle

---

[1] A. J. Swinney, *Museum Accreditation* (Washington, D. C., 1978) p. 9.

class audience but all its audiences. In 1971, the AAM published a report, *Museums: Their New Audience,* that urged museums to place greater budgetary importance upon the areas of education and community relations and to begin a search for new and non-traditional audiences. Museums were mandated to serve a broader cross section of their publics, and those publics stood ready to hold them accountable.

In response to public pressure, museums have made an effort to integrate themselves more fully into the total fabric of American life. In their attempts to serve the total community, museums provide not only programming events for the general public but also special programs specifically structured for audiences such as the handicapped, preschoolers, children, ethnic groups, senior citizens, adults, and members. Today's museums are largely activity centers where the visitor, in addition to viewing exhibits, can participate in numerous educational experiences, including seminars and workshops, theatre performances, lectures, film series, guided visits, and demonstrations. This program diversity resulted from the conscious decision by museums to extend their services to a more heterogeneous audience.

Museums are currently enjoying an attendance boom: a recent poll for the Institute of Museum Services by the National Center for Educational Statistics indicates that museum visitation increased by 50 million during the period from 1975 through 1979.[2] No longer viewed as elitist, museums are seen as institutions for everyone. A number of factors have contributed to this increase in attendance. First, there has been an active attempt on the part of museums to increase their public appeal through expanded educational programming, more hands-on exhibits encouraging visitor participation, and the mounting of *blockbuster* exhibits that have immense popular appeal, such as the Treasures of Tutankhamen. The second factor is the change in the profile of the general population. Increased leisure time and mobility coupled with higher educational achievement have prompted people to frequent museums in search of recreation and educa-

---

[2]National Center for Educational Statistics, *1979 Museum Program Survey* (November, 1980).

tion. The final contributing factor is the expanded media coverage of museum events via newspapers, magazines, television, and radio.

There are many different types of museums, including youth museums, neighborhood museums, science centers, historical houses and villages, zoos, art, and natural science museums. They vary in size of staff, budgets, attendance, audiences, and program scope. Some emphasize aesthetics; some are concerned with the learning process; others strive to be community centers. However, there are some common characteristics that all museums share. All museums are not-for-profit institutions that are open to the public. Concerned with improving the quality of their visitor's educational and recreational experiences, they attempt to increase awareness, generate thought and develop new interests among their visitors. However, their primary function is to collect, preserve, research, and exhibit artifacts for educational purposes. Indeed, this is the one function that is unique to the museum and cannot be duplicated by any other institutions.

In 1979, after experiencing guided visits at the Indianapolis Children's Museum, kindergarten and primary students were asked to tell what they thought a museum was. They described a museum as, "A place where they could learn and have fun at the same time!" "A place to see things that you have never seen before." "A place that saves things. A place for big people too!" "A place where you can learn how things were a long time ago."

MUSEUM EDUCATION

Museum education is different from traditional schooling. It is noncompulsory, informal education relying on none of the controls of grades, tests, and legal restrictions that characterize learning in the schools. The visitor is free to come and go at will, exploring the exhibits at his own pace and according to his interests. Museum visitors must be attracted, stimulated, and persuaded to look at exhibits and consider their implications.[3] Because museum learning is voluntary, it must be a pleasurable ex-

---

[3]Douglas Allen, "The Museum and Its Functions," *The Organization of Museums — Practical Advice* (Paris, 1960), p. 25.

perience, if the visitor is to continue to partake. Learning in the museum is largely visual, in contrast to the classroom, where the emphasis is upon books and words as a way of learning. In the museum environment, the specimens and their interpretation by way of exhibits and docents are the focus. Museums are an important adjunct to formal education, but they are far more interested in awakening the visitor's interest and curiosity and helping him to develop some ideas on a subject rather than in indoctrinating him with factual information. Among the prime goals of museum education is the stimulation of the visitor's imagination and the development of his sensory awareness.[4] Learning is viewed by museum educators as an open-ended, ongoing, life-long experience. The Institute of Museum Services poll indicated that more than two-thirds of all canvassed museums ranked education as a high priority activity.[5] Museums are committed to providing continuous education for the entire community, and every effort is made to encourage repeat visits by their audiences.

To fulfill their educational function, museums must attempt to communicate some information to the visitor through their exhibits, since communication is the essential element in interpretation. Gabriel Cherem, in his paper *The Environmental Interpreter: New Frontiers,* states that interpretation consists of three components:

1. An on-the-site activity occurring in museums, historic sites, etc.
2. Informal education with a voluntary, noncaptive audience
3. A motivational rather than factual approach[6]

THE DOCENT

The docent represents an extension of the interpretive function and attempts to make a particular exhibit more meaningful

---

[4]Hiroshi Daifuku, "The Museum and the Visitor," *The Organization of Museums – Practical Advice* (Paris, 1960), p. 83.

[5]National Center for Educational Statistics, *1979 Museum Program Survey* (November, 1980).

[6]Gabriel Cherem, *The Environmental Interpreter: New Frontiers* (National Bridge, Virginia, 1975) p. 3.

for a person or group, through the sharing of information. Functioning as a teacher, as a facilitator, and as an interpreter, the docent uses exhibits to educate. The docent's role within the museum is a multidimensional one. He is a representative of the museum who tries to make the visitor's museum visit memorable and rewarding. The docent is not only an interpreter of exhibits but also a public relations person who embodies the museum's professionalism, sensitivity, and social awareness, or the lack of it, in his interaction with the public.

Certainly the docent must possess a sound factual foundation and a familiarity and thorough understanding of the museum's collections and exhibits, as this constitutes the basis for structuring tours and successfully utilizing the various interpretive techniques. However, if the docent is to be effective there are some other equally important characteristics and personality traits that must be present. The docent must sincerely enjoy meeting and working with people and have good communication skills. He must be patient, flexible, perceptive, and responsive to people. This enthusiasm for the public must be complemented with an equally intense enthusiasm for the museum. The docent must have a sincere love of learning and a commitment to ongoing training and be both imaginative and creative in his museum teaching. However, the docent is not omniscient and should never hesitate to admit when he doesn't know.

DOCENT TRAINING

With the increased emphasis upon professionalism, museums can no longer permit their docent programs total autonomy. Rather, there has to be a staff supervisor responsible for the program, clearly defined program goals and objectives, and a structured training program that provides docents with the needed skills and insights to implement the program directives. The museums should furnish their docents with an explicit statement defining and delineating their interpretive role and realm of responsibility and accountability. The training is an attempt by the museum to establish consistent interpretive goals and levels of performance and to eliminate the perpetuation of fabrication

and erroneous information among the docents. The following key components should be a part of the training program:
- Lectures presenting factual and background information
- Workshops emphasizing interpretive techniques, such as questioning skills
- Gallery visits providing information about specific objects and exhibits
- Guided visit observations enabling the docents to observe the application of the training
- Book lists for supplementary reading
- Written resource information for reference purposes

The training should also help the docent understand the mechanics of moving groups from exhibit to exhibit, controlling group behavior, and implementing safety and emergency procedures. In order that docents may keep abreast of current information and interpretive techniques, the museum must continue to provide ongoing training for them.

RECRUITMENT

Docents may be either men or women, paid staff or volunteers. While it is true that paid staff docents mean greater control, reliability, and performance uniformity for the museum, most docent programs consist predominantly of volunteers. A docent's volunteer status does not minimize his responsibility to the museum to perform as a professional. Participation in the program demands a commitment of time, effort, and adherence to program dictates that must be met. How does the museum find volunteers possessing the personality traits, enthusiasm, and commitment essential to effective docentry? Newspapers, television, radio public service spots, member newsletters, clubs and organizations, intern programs, and even the docent programs are excellent recruitment vehicles. Prospective docents should be interviewed by the museum staff volunteer coordinator and/or the supervisor of the docent program. At that time the program philosophy, role of the docent, and the training and program requirements should be explained to the interviewee.

There should be a mutually beneficial relationship that exists between the museum and the volunteer docent. The museum acquires unpaid personnel to implement and augment its interpretive program, while participation in the program for the volunteer brings personal satisfaction, growth, and new friendships. The volunteer docent expects the museum to provide an effective training program, a well-organized interpretive program, and efficient scheduling procedures. The museum should establish some expressions of appreciation for the docent's volunteer efforts. Luncheons, certificates, plaques, gift shop discounts, and other privileges are forms of recognition. If the volunteer/museum relationship is to work, there must be a designated staff member who works closely with the volunteers and assumes responsibility for the interpretive program and to whom the docent looks for direction and guidance.

INTERPRETATION

All of the docent's efforts as an interpreter are aimed at trying to make information about the past understandable in relation to the present.[7] As a facilitator, the docent provides the visitor with some assistance in educating himself. Using the inquiry method the docent employs questioning as a means of helping the visitor to sharpen his observation and analytical skills. Stressing that information is not static, he encourages a plurality of responses rather than a single response among the group. The docent de-emphasizes *telling* information; instead the visitor is urged to look to an exhibit, object, or personal experience for an explanation. The visitor is motivated by the docent to be an active participant, that is a seeker rather than a passive receiver of information. The docent does not judge the quality of the ideas expressed by the visitors but must help them clarify and broaden their thinking. Not only must the docent evoke, he must also respond to the visitor's curiosity.

Thus, an important part of the docent's role is to help the visitor critically examine and analyze museum objects and exhibits for information. Most people come to museums, excluding art museums, conditioned to consider the printed exhibit label as the primary source of information. Visitors must also be trained to view objects as equally important sources of information. Questioning is a most effective way of directing the visitor's attention

---

[7] Richard Vandeway, *Planning Museum Tours* (Nashville, 1977), p. 4.

to the object. The following are some essential questions to be asked about the object: What is the object? From what material is it made? How was it made? How does it work? How was it used? Who made the object? What skills were needed?

In addition to focusing upon the object as an isolated entity, the technical leaflet *Planning Museum Tours* discusses two other levels of object interpretation. The object can be placed within its context of time and place and critically examined for the information it reveals about the owner's life and the broader culture.[8] The object may tell about the life-styles of the people, their beliefs, habits, and aspirations. It might represent a particular historical period or event; it might be an example of a lost craft or skill; or it might represent the introduction of technology that greatly altered the culture. The object can also be a frame of reference that allows the visitor to compare and contrast it with his own time and place and determine the similarities, differences, and changes.[9] The successful *reading* of museum objects heightens the visitor's visual awareness and requires that he use his skills of observation, comparison, reasoning, and judging.

THE GUIDED VISIT

The guided visit is a fluid, organic presentation that derives its form from the audience. The docent's prime responsibility is to adapt the format of the visit to the interests, experiences, and background of each different group of visitors. When structuring the visit, the docent is concerned with fulfilling three goals: providing the visitor with an enjoyable museum experience, helping the visitor to understand what a museum is and how it is different from other institutions, and promoting return visits. To accomplish these goals the docent must refrain from overstructuring the visit but must instead stand ready to improvise and modify in keeping with the group's needs and wishes. The docent must involve the visitor in active mental and physical participation throughout the visit. Such activities as questioning, observing activities, games, tactile experiences, role playing, improvisation, and body movement are effective ways of involving the visitor. When deciding what is to be accomplished during the visit,

---

[8]Ibid, p. 4.
[9]Ibid, p. 4.

the docent must remember to limit the scope of the ideas and concepts to be developed. It is important to remember that even a guided group must be given opportunities to freely explore exhibits at their own pace and according to their own interests.

GUIDED VISIT OBJECTIVES

The establishment of goals and objectives contribute to the following:
— Program direction, priority, and focus
— Decision making
— Program evaluation
— Program accountability

Goals are broad, general statements of purpose derived from the museum's philosophy. In contrast, objectives are specific performance tasks and behaviors structured to achieve the goal statements. Objectives help the docent to focus the interpretive interactions, increase learning efficiency, and evaluate audience response. There are three elements to the well-constructed objective:
— Learning — What are you trying to teach?
— Activity — How are you going to teach it?
— Evaluation — Did you teach it?

Objectives should be
— Precise, clear statements telling what will be done
— Achievable
— Compatible with goals
— Meaningful — something you believe important to achieve

Objectives form the planning base for interpretative activities. Once an objective has been decided upon, the docent must determine the most effective means of accomplishing it via museum exhibits.

Objectives reflect three areas of learning: the cognitive domain concerned with intellectual achievement, the affective domain synonymous with feeling and attitudes, and the psychomotor domain, which is the physical, manipulative, and motor realm. Attitudes are slow to change and learning in the affective domain is difficult to attain. To achieve affective objectives the docent must

— Indicate the attitudes and values that are to be changed
— Structure learning experiences that will lead to the development of those attitudes and values
— Become aware of the group's attitudes and values
— Remain impartial

THE AUDIENCE OF THE GUIDED VISIT

While there are distinct differences among the various audiences a docent encounters on a guided visit, there are also some common characteristics. As a rule, the docent rarely speaks to the same audience twice, instead the docent meets new and different groups daily. Museum audiences vary in age, economic and social background, interests, experiences, values, and viewpoints. But in spite of this diversity, the docent must familiarize himself with the audience's concerns and needs. Freeman Tilden in his book *Interpreting Our Heritage* says that "the visitor ultimately is seeing things through his own eyes, not those of the interpreter, and he is finally translating your words as best he can into whatever he can refer to in his intimate knowledge and experience."[10] Every effort must be made by the docent to view the subject from the perspective of the audience and to incorporate the audience's expectations and perceptions into the visit format. The docent should draw upon the visitor's knowledge, experiences, and perceptions to help interpret the museum objects and exhibits and unconditionally accept the visitor's point of view. Every effort must be made to clearly understand the *why* behind the visitor's response and to see the question, issue, or situation from his point of view. Carl Rogers says that "the separateness of individuals, the right of each individual to utilize his experience in his own way and to discover his own meanings in it — this is one of the most priceless potentialities of life."[11]

The size of the group will also influence what happens on a guided visit, as the number of persons in a group and the spatial size of the area within which the docent must work affect and finally control the types of interpretive activities he can engage in.

---

[10] Freeman Tilden, *Interpreting Our Heritage* (Chapel Hill, 1974), p. 14.
[11] Carl Rogers, *On Becoming A Person* (Boston, 1961), p. 21.

The type of group, whether it is a club, scout group, school class, family, church or camp group, determines the tone and focus of the program. In essence, the docent must structure a guided visit that will have broad interest and appeal for the greatest number of individuals among his audience.

As a rule, a docent works with either groups of children or adults or sometimes a combination of both. To competently work with either of these audiences in interpretive interactions, the docent must have a clear understanding of the characteristics that make each unique from the other. While adult attendance is a personal, voluntary choice, a child's museum attendance is usually mandatory and outside his control, determined by either his parents, teacher, or some other adult. Educational psychologists have learned that children are fundamentally different from adults in their perceptions of the world and their physical capabilities. Furthermore, their growth is along comparatively set, developmental sequences that greatly influence their behavior and learning capabilities. Adult personal development is not static but ongoing and is often the impetus for continuous education and training. Both adults and children learn best when they are cosharers of experiences and information. Children especially need active learning situations that encourage hands-on experiences. Adults bring to a learning situation numerous life experiences that contribute to a personal sense of history. In contrast, children have limited life experiences and little personal history. Adults are independent, self-directed learners who seek an instantaneous use of information. On the other hand, children frequently learn information that has no immediate use in their life. Adults also demand greater accountability from the museum for the success or failure of its programs than children.

In conclusion, the museum is a dynamic, vibrant institution with a vital role to play in the community. It is an institution that seeks to serve the public by preserving society's material culture and helping man to become a more aware, discerning, and sensitive human being. The museum offers its visitors an affirmation through its specimens of man's ingenuity, resourcefulness, and longevity. It provides a linkage with the past and insight into the future for its visitors. It is a place where the public can engage in numerous activities providing purposeful and personally rewarding leisure time experiences.

The docent is an integral part of the museum's interpretive function. His role is to help the visitor to utilize the museum in the most personally meaningful way and to share not only factual information but a unique way of *seeing.* For above all else the museum is a visual experience. The docent's excitement, professionalism, love of people, and respect for learning can be translated into a most memorable and pleasurable experience for the visitor. As a representative of the museum, the docent can emulate all that is good about the museum and help create lifelong museum visitors and program participants.

Chapter 2

INQUIRY EDUCATIONAL METHODS

That I be not a restless ghost who haunts your footsteps
as they pass. . . You must be free to take a path
whose end I feel no need to know. . .
Margaret Mead, 1947

IN recent years, museum education researchers have found
that guided tours can be more than simply a *show-and-tell*
lecture with no participation on the part of the people involved
in the tour. Evidence collected during guided tours indicates that
inquiry educational methods radically improve the quality and
quantity of the museum visit. Inquiry methods contain many
unique elements, but once they become incorporated into the
educational programs of the museum, they are easily retained via
the docent training programs.

To illustrate the elements of inquiry we can begin with a
statement that may have been presented by a docent to a tour
group. *This is a photograph of a steamboat invented by Robert
Fulton in 1807.* This is a statement of *fact*, and we can test you
on this statement by asking the two-part question, *Who invented
the steamboat, and in what year was it invented?* As long as your
memory records *Robert Fulton* and *1807* you will answer this
question correctly. However, research indicates that low level
memory information such as this is easily forgotten (usually
within twenty-four hours). There are several reasons for this, including the fact that material such as this has been imposed upon
the learner and the learner neither understands this information

nor desires it. As a result, when the learner forgets the proposition about the steamboat he has nothing left from his museum experience — his educational residue is zero. The principle reason for this lack of educational residue is that he has had no direct sensory experience in finding out about Robert Fulton, about steamboats, and about the year 1807.

Now, contrast the foregoing procedure for learning this historical idea with the following:

> As we board the model of the steamboat built in 1807, you will need to use your senses (sight, sound, smell, touch, and taste) to record your experiences. How did you feel when the bell sounded? The steam rushed out of the boiler? The paddle wheel began to turn? John Fitch invented the steamboat about twenty years earlier than Robert Fulton. See if you can find out why John Fitch was ignored and died penniless while Robert Fulton received the credit in all the history books.

We need to recognize that if the museum visitor becomes directly involved in the museum visit through the use of the senses and then is encouraged to go further, the visitor will be developing his rational powers (his ability to think). That development will take place because the visitor must actually collect and classify data, compare classifications, synthesize an answer to the question based upon the data, and ultimately take a stand on the question, which is based upon what he truly believes and not upon what someone has told him. In this type of learning situation, the visitor is developing his own rational powers, and he is simultaneously developing an understanding of the content involved because he is evolving the content as he works. The museum visitor is also learning how to find out information that he does not have and increasing his confidence in his ability to inquire; in short, the museum visitor is learning how to learn — the ultimate goal of museum education.

Docents must recognize and receive instruction in the differences between authoritative and inquiry museum learning. Authoritative docents prescribe the material to be covered and dictate the manner in which it is to be learned. This results in very little retention of the material and usually a negative attitude toward museums and the museum tour. An alternative is to utilize

```
CONVERGENT THINKING QUESTION----------------------DEVELOPS ONE RIGHT ANSWER


DIVERGENT THINKING QUESTION-----------------------DEVELOPS MANY RIGHT ANSWERS
```

Figure 2-1.

TABLE 2-I

CONVERGENT THINKING	VS	DIVERGENT THINKING
1. Docent focuses upon learning <u>right</u> answers.		1. Docent focuses upon developing the visitor's own answers.
2. Answers are <u>documented</u> by authoritative sources such as the docent.		2. Answers are based upon a visitor's ideas and research.
3. Docent focuses upon finding the <u>right</u> answers.		3. Docent focuses upon building reasons for answers.
4. Docent seeks agreement in answering questions.		4. Docent encourages disagreement and discussion to clarify issues.
5. Docent answers tend to give facts and explain systems.		5. Docent answers tend to analyze and evaluate systems.
6. Docent does not require original thoughts from the visitors.		6. Docent encourages and requires original thoughts from the visitors.

inquiry instruction as the vehicle whereby the docent involves the museum visitors in the tour through questioning and assisting only when deemed necessary. As a result, content is learned, but the *method* that the docent uses enables the museum visitor to achieve more than content understanding; he also develops his ability to think.

CONVERGENT VERSUS DIVERGENT THINKING

When developing the thinking ability of museum patrons through tours or during individual visitations, it is best to focus upon divergent rather than convergent thinking. As shown in Figure 2-1, the main difference between convergent and divergent thinking lies in the development of answers to questions. Table 2-I summarizes the differences between convergent and divergent thinking as related to questioning.

Divergent thinking also encourages the use of five processes that result in the development of open-ended questions that are asked by docents: fluency, flexibility, originality, elaboration, and evaluation. Fluency refers to the development of many responses for a given situation. Here the emphasis is upon quantity rather than the quality of the response. Thus, the more responses given to the docent by the tour group the better. The following are statements that encourage fluency:

1. List many ways to. . .
2. Think of several possible ways to. . .
3. Come up with ideas for. . .

Flexibility results when the docent develops thinking in a variety of categories by shifting thinking from one approach into many different avenues or ways of thinking. Flexibility can be developed using statements such as the following:

1. List many different ways to. . .
2. Think of different ways to. . .
3. What are the different types of. . .

Originality involves the development of unusual or uncommon responses that utilize clever and unique ideas that are relevant but away from the obvious. Originality can be fostered using statements such as the following:

1. Think of ideas that no one else in the group will think of related to. . .
2. Think of unique and unusual ways to. . .

Elaboration involves the addition of details to a basic idea to make it more interesting and complete. Docent statements such as those that follow help foster elaboration:

1. Add supplemental ideas to make the basic idea clearer.
2. Think of details to add to your main idea.

Evaluation, one of the most important attributes of divergent thinking, involves the weighing of ideas in terms of the idea's desirability and undesirability. Statements such as the following are used to foster evaluation:

1. List the things that you like and dislike about. . .
2. List the pros and cons of. . .

For evaluation, it is important that the docent develop an equal number of likes and dislikes or pros and cons in order to remain neutral on the object or event being discussed. The visitors should be allowed and encouraged to formulate their own conclusions rather than that of the docent.

WAIT TIME AND ITS EFFECTS

Suppose you were part of a museum tour group and you spent the entire tour listening to the docent lecture about various exhibits. Then suppose that the docent asked the tour group two or three questions per minute allowing less than one second for a response before asking the next question. How would you feel about this machine gun approach to questioning?

What if, on the other hand, docents posed challenging questions (divergent, of course) and then paused for at least six seconds after asking the question to give people time to think about an answer? Research results indicate that this technique alone can increase the number of evaluative questions visitors ask by up to seven or eight times when compared to earlier tours. Furthermore, instead of losing visitors (a common occurrence on guided tours) new people were attracted to the tour and more discussion prevailed among members of the tour.[1]

---

[1] Alicia Fortinberry, "The Art of Piquing Art Questions," *Psychology Today*, April, 1980, pp. 30, 33.

Docents should be encouraged to begin tours by informing visitors that this tour will not be a straight lecture, but rather an exciting alternative that is purposely intended to stimulate questions:

1. Why do you think they placed this object in this museum?
2. What feelings does this exhibit or work arouse in you?

Docents then must remember to wait at least six to eight seconds for a response and to involve as many visitors as possible in the response as shown in Figure 2-2. The main difference as shown in Figure 2-2 is that of visitor involvement. Instead of the docent conversing with one visitor the docent is now interacting with many visitors.

Additional stimulating questions might also include the following:

1. Why should paintings like this be kept in a museum? Who decides and why?
2. How does one decide what belongs in this museum?
3. Here is a new aquisition for our museum. Tell me where you think we should locate it and why.

Wait time used in conjunction with inquiry-oriented tours will result in the following positive changes in visitors:

1. Visitor responses to docent questions will increase dramatically.
2. The number of unsolicited but appropriate responses by visitors will increase.
3. Failure by visitors to respond will decrease.
4. Visitor confidence and enjoyment with the museum visit will increase.
5. Higher level inquiry and divergent thinking will be increased.
6. Docent-visitor interaction will increase along with the interaction between visitors.
7. The number of questions asked by visitors will increase.
8. Contributions by normally *quiet* or *shy* visitors will increase as people begin to feel that their questions are welcome and that their questions are valued by the docent tour leader.
9. Guided tours will gain visitors rather than lose them as in

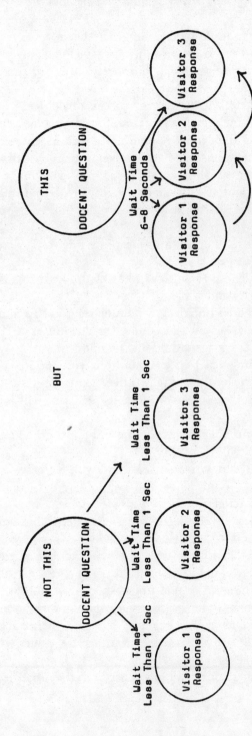

Figure 2-2. Increasing Visitor Responses to Docent Questions

the past when visitors became disinterested as the tour progressed.

Positive changes in docents will also be observed using these methods:

1. Docent responses to visitor questions will exhibit a greater flexibility and variety of responses as wait time increases and as visitors receive encouragement.

2. The number and type of questions docents ask on guided tours will improve. Number of machine-gun type questions will decrease as the docent wait time and visitor interaction increases. The number of higher level thinking questions will increase, and there will be a decrease in low level memory recall questions.

3. Docents will feel more positive as partners in the questioning process and will develop to their fullest instead of spouting off the same canned material to every visitor group. As a result, visitors will want more guided tours, not less, and will appreciate each docent as a unique person with something positive to offer.

4. More people will want to become docents under this *new* wait time and inquiry format.

5. Docents will move from the role of lecturer to the role of a participating observer. They will also observe objects as the group observes them. Remember, the eyes of a group of preschoolers will observe different things than the eyes of a visiting basketball team.

LEVELS OF QUESTIONING

There is a direct relationship between questioning level and the level of inquiry fostered by docents. As a result, it is important for docents to recognize that questions do fall into categories and that one's questions can be analyzed and evaluated according to predetermined designated levels. Table 2-II illustrates one way of classifying questions into levels. In order to adequately identify questioning levels, we will consider each level individually and include examples of questions that reflect that level. It is of immense value for docents to prepare their own questions

TABLE 2-II

LEVELS OF QUESTIONING

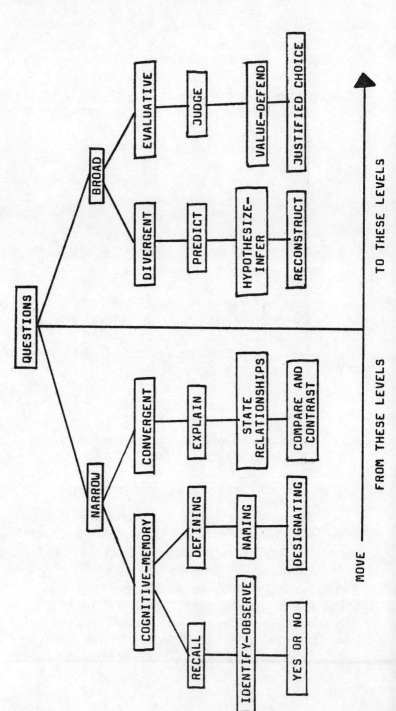

by level in order to reflect how easy it is to prepare narrow, cognitive memory-convergent questions and how much more time consuming and difficult it is to prepare broad, divergent evaluative questions. It is also important for docents to consider the following questions as they prepare their own questions to ask visitors:

1. Why do you ask visitors questions?
2. What do you expect from a question?
3. What do you want a question to do for your guided tour?
4. What kind(s) of questions should be asked?
5. When do you ask questions on a guided tour?
6. How do you ask visitors questions?

Sample responses from docents who utilize inquiry tours and ask higher level questions include the following:

1. Why do you ask visitors questions?
   a. To start visitors thinking.
   b. To see if the visitor is thinking about an exhibit.
   c. To invite visitor participation.
   d. To create interest.
   e. To find out what the tour group knows about a particular exhibit before beginning the tour.
   f. To help visitors develop self-confidence.
2. What do you expect from a question?
   a. An honest reply.
   b. A response that leaves both the docent and the visitor free to ask another question (thus questions that invite a yes or no answer are of limited value).
   c. An opportunity for a visitor to ask his own question.
3. What do you want a question to do for your guided tour?
   a. Free a visitor to ask questions.
   b. Personally involve the visitor.
   c. Stimulate interaction among the visitors.
   d. Lead to further involvement in an exhibit.
4. What kind(s) of questions should be asked?
   a. One in which the visitor believes that the answer is important.
   b. One that stimulates additional inquiry.
   c. A question that can be built upon by the visitors.

     d. A question that is not misleading to visitors.

     e. *Why* questions should be used sparingly, since they can be indefinite, instead of asking why something happened or is there, ask the visitor what evidence he can give that something happened or is true.

  5. When do you ask a question?

     a. When you want the visitor to move on to another exhibit area.

     b. To get the visitors back on the track or away from a dead end.

     c. To ascertain the visitor's understanding of an exhibit area.

     d. To stimulate group discussion.

     e. To focus attention on visitor inquiry from the very beginning.

     f. To find out what the visitor is doing and thinking.

  6. How do you ask visitors questions?

     a. Ask with enthusiasm and genuine interest, but easily and informally.

     b. Make sure that you ask the question first, select the respondent, and then have two or three additional persons also respond to the same question.

     c. Don't rush the person to respond.

     d. Encourage the visitors to listen carefully to the question and then to volunteer answers.

Cognitive memory questions (*see* Table 2-II) are the narrowest type of questions asked and require only the lowest level of thought on the part of the museum visitor. Cognitive memory questions require recall, memory, recognition, and descriptions of previously obtained factual knowledge or observation. These questions call for predictable responses and often demand one word answers by the visitor. After four weeks have elapsed and under the most favorable conditions, retention of answers based upon cognitive memory questions is estimated to be at a 35 percent retention rate.

The following are examples of cognitive memory questions:

1. What is gravity? (Define)
2. Who took this photograph? (Name)
3. What kind of nut is this? (Recall)

4. Is this a thermometer? (Yes - No)

5. How many people do you see? (Observe)

Notice that all of the questions require a low level of thinking on the part of the visitor and that responses from all visitors would virtually be identical.

Convergent questions require that facts be combined to obtain one right answer. The visitor must know facts and explain concepts, describe interrelationships, and make comparisons. The level of thinking required for convergent questions is at a higher level than that required by cognitive memory questions.

The following are sample convergent questions:

1. What does the turtle do? (Explain)
2. How is this photograph like that one? (Compare and contrast)
3. How do the horse and dragonlike animals differ? (State relationships)
4. What is for sale in this store? (Explain)

Retention of answers to convergent questions, after four weeks has elapsed and under the most favorable conditions, is estimated to be about 50 percent.

Divergent questions provide the museum visitor with a new situation and also allow for more than one possible right answer. These are questions that permit originality by the respondee as evidenced by the hypotheses made and in the way he uses his knowledge to solve new problems. Divergent questions also permit predicting, inferring, and reconstruction of events:

1. Who can predict the next portrait in this exhibit? (Predict)
2. If the dinosaur did not have all these body parts, what would he do to move from one location to another (Inferring)
3. Demonstrate how this photograph was taken. (Reconstruct)
4. Why do you think that the boat would not float? (Hypothesize)

Retention of answers to divergent questions, after four weeks has elapsed and under the most favorable conditions, is estimated to be about 80 percent. Notice how the rate of retention of material elicited by higher level questions increases as one moves from narrow to broad questions.

Evaluative questions constitute the highest level of questioning. They require the museum visitor to judge, value, defend, or justify a choice. Evaluative questions require the respondee to organize knowledge, formulate an opinion, take a position, use evidence, make a judgment, use criteria, and develop standards of judgment. The retention of answers given to evaluative questions is estimated to be at the 95 percent level under the most favorable conditions.

1. What do you think about this painting? (Judge)
2. Do you agree that this is the best exhibit in the museum? (Justified choice)
3. What is your reaction to the inner city exhibit? (Value - Defend)
4. Of all the contributions that Thomas Edison made to the advancement of our society, which do you think serves us best today? (Justified choice)

ATTITUDINAL QUESTIONS

Developing positive attitudes for visitors is extremely important since once an attitude is fostered about a particular person, place, or object, that attitude is very difficult to change. Visitors that develop a negative attitude toward a museum visit, guided tour, or docent may not wish to return to the museum for another visit. Furthermore, they can influence their friends with respect to future museum visits. Therefore, it behooves all museum personnel to foster positive attitudes toward the museum visit since with positive attitudes comes museum support (financial and voluntary) from the community that is served. Attitudes that are desirable to foster include the following:

1. Curiosity
2. Inventiveness
3. Critical thinking
4. Persistence

Curiosity involves using as many senses as possible to explore an object or event. Encouraging involvement in a particular event, Energy Day, for example, is one aspect of curiosity. Encouraging the asking of questions also helps to promote curiosity.

Inventiveness involves the generation of new ideas that result in the development of original thinking. Inventiveness involves the use of exhibits in a novel or unique manner and encourages the use of novel conclusions based upon observations.

Critical thinking involves the use of sound reasons when giving suggestions, conclusions, or when making predictions. Visitors should be encouraged to use observable evidence to justify their conclusions, to predict the outcome of events, to justify their predictions in terms of past experiences, to change their ideas in response to evidence or to logical reasons, to point out contradictions in the evidence being presented, and to interpret observations.

Persistence should be encouraged in visitors to assist them in understanding the many, many hours it takes to prepare an exhibit that the average person will view for two minutes. Visitors should be encouraged to evaluate exhibits by being encouraged to return to exhibits to obtain new information or to view an exhibit from a different perspective. They should also be exposed to the time frame that the exhibit or event dipicts. How long did the War of 1812 last? How long did it take Lewis and Clark to complete their trip? How long do the astronauts spend preparing for that one ride in the space shuttle? How long does it take for an artist to become *famous*? Visitors can develop totally new understandings and a positive attitude when evidence of persistence is also included in the tour of exhibit explanation. Persistence leads to success and success leads to positive attitudes, which result in a continual return to the museum for further learning.

CRITERIA FOR EFFECTIVELY PHRASED QUESTIONS

Effectively phrased questions can also enhance the success of a tour and lead to greater discussion and involvement on the part of the participants. Effectively phrased questions often have one or more of the following characteristics:

1. They are creative and imaginative and cause the person responding to move out into new areas.
2. They require that individual elements be put together into new patterns by the person.
3. They call for making predictions or formulating hypotheses.
4. They call for making inferences.

5. They are geared to the audience participating in the tour, i.e. different terminology, analogies, or examples for different age levels — such as preschool versus senior citizen groups.
6. They encourage the association of ideas by calling for comparisons of previously unrelated objects.
7. They are clearly stated using a distinct word order.
8. They encourage responses that are usually unpredictable because their open-ended nature encourages several alternative responses.
9. They are usually part of a planned sequence requiring higher level thought processes and are based upon the answers of the visitors.

WORKSHOPS FOR DOCENTS

As you can tell from the heavy emphasis that this chapter has placed upon inquiry tours and questioning, workshops for docents are essential. Many of the ideas presented in this chapter can be used to develop a meaningful workshop for docents. Ideally, at least two three-hour sessions as a minimum should be devoted to assisting docents in the development of an effective inquiry and questioning skills format. As part of the workshop, docents should be assigned the development of questions by level, and they should be encouraged to develop higher level divergent questions. Docent question cards (Figure 2-3) are an excellent method for involving docents in the process of preparing inquiry-oriented questions. The questions can be collected, assimilated, and then made available to all docents for consideration for use with their tours. This will result in the development of a cadre of questions that can be made available to all present and future docents. Eventually, a superb questioning repertoire can be developed.

While most museums place a great deal of emphasis upon the knowledge acquired by docents via workshops conducted by content specialist, an *equal* emphasis must also be placed upon the acquisition of methods and techniques. Otherwise, the content tour will be doomed to failure. Furthermore, docents must understand that a one to three hour workshop dealing with the topic of dinosaurs is no substitute for people who have devoted

Go to the _____ area.

(Insert name of area docent should proceed to.)

In the space below, write one cognitive-memory, one convergent, two divergent, and two evaluative questions that you could use with a tour group. Make sure that your questions encourage the development of curiosity, inventiveness, critical thinking, and persistence on the part of the tour group.

Figure 2-3. Docent Question Card

their life to the study of dinosaurs. That is why the workshop devoted to methods and techniques is as important as, or even more important than, the content workshop portion. A docent trained in inquiry and questioning can find out answers to content when needed. A content-oriented docent can neither remember the content nor impart it effectively for lasting value that will foster life long learning. Thus, the minimum docent workshop should be broken down into thirds as shown in Figure 2-4.

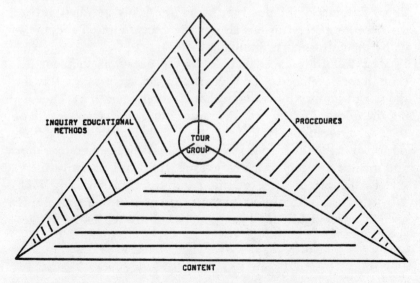

Figure 2-4. Docent Workshop Triangle

THE GUIDED VISIT

The introduction to a guided visit is extremely important since it sets the tone for the entire tour. When introducing the guided visit, it is usually worthwhile to set the stage for the visit by informing the visitors of the goals and objectives of the visit. The overall goals and objectives may have already been determined by the group, i.e. a Scout troop wants to learn about airplanes; they may have been partially determined and need refining by the docent; or they need to be totally developed during the initial few minutes prior to the tour. Visitors should be informed of the characteristics of the tour, the methods of questioning and inquiry to be used, areas to be visited, wait time technique, and the overall role of the docent. Visitors should be encouraged and told that they are invited and welcome to participate in the tour and that there will be many opportunities for involvement.

EVALUATING THE INQUIRY TOUR DOCENT

There are several recommended guidelines that can be used to evaluate the success of the inquiry tour. A sample evaluation is included in Table 2-III and may be adapted to fit individual situations. Evaluations of this type should not only be filled out by the docent's supervisor but also by the docent himself and, ideally, by the visitors participating in the tour.

The following pages include sample questions that our docents have developed. These questions can serve as starters for the use of inquiry tours that utilize divergent questions. Then using the docent question card your docents can develop a cadre of their own questions. Notice that these questions follow the criteria for divergent questions indicated in this chapter and that they also include a variety of learning levels. It might be worthwhile to select a sample of these questions for classification using Table 2-II. Also notice that most of these questions are general enough so that any exhibit or object can be substituted into the question.

SAMPLE DOCENT QUESTIONS

1. Who can explain what all these objects are used for?
2. How are these objects similar?

TABLE 2-III

THE INQUIRY TOUR DOCENT CHECKLIST

Directions

Place a check (✓) in one box after each statement.

As our docent, you:

		4 ALL OF THE TIME	3 MOST OF THE TIME	2 SOME OF THE TIME	1 NEVER	DOES NOT APPLY
1.	Explain things clearly.					
2.	Give explanations that we understand					
3.	Allow us to conclude for ourselves.					
4.	Are not afraid to say "I don't know."					
5.	Do not tell us everything about the exhibit.					
6.	Make us feel that our explanations are good ones.					
7.	Listen to our responses.					
8.	Encourage visitor interaction.					
9.	Are flexible when conducting the tour.					
10.	Are not too quick to give the "right" answer.					
11.	Wait long enough for us to think of our own answers.					
12.	Ask questions that make us think.					
13.	Make your questions clear, concise, and to the point.					
14.	Explain with examples.					
15.	Do not let the clock govern your tour.					

TABLE 2-III (continued)

	4 ALL OF THE TIME	3 MOST OF THE TIME	2 SOME OF THE TIME	1 NEVER	DOES NOT APPLY
16. Make us want to return for another tour with you.					
Supervisors and docents may want to add these questions to the evaluation form:					
17. Ask the tour group what they know about the topic or exhibit before giving your explanation.					
18. Wait more than three seconds for a response.					
19. Develop visitor-visitor interaction rather than docent-visitor interaction.					
20. Ask affective (attitudinal) questions.					
21. Reinforce a visitor's answer without simply saying that the response is correct.					
22. Do not stop the discussion about an exhibit or object when the right answer is given, but ask if there are other answers.					
23. Ask questions requiring thinking.					
24. Listen to what the visitor has to say.					
25. Ask divergent questions.					
26. Do not interrupt visitors before they have completed their responses.					

3. How are these objects different?
4. What do you think happened to the dinosaurs that would cause them to not be found on the Earth today?
5. From observing the tomb, can someone interpret how they think the Egyptians felt about death?
6. Pretend that you could travel with the aid of a time machine back to ancient Egypt to meet a person your age. What would you ask him? What would you want him to know about you?
7. Observe the hieroglyphics on the tomb wall. Pretend that you are a secret agent trying to decode these messages. What do you think the message is?
8. How is a soft-shelled turtle like a hard-shelled turtle? How are they different?
9. Scientists call turtles *living fossils*. Why would they use this term?
10. Observe the 1890 firehouse. What features do you observe that are like our fire stations today and what features are different? What will the fire stations of the twenty-first century be like?
11. Classify the fire hoses. Why would there be different types of fire hoses?
12. If you were living on the third floor of a house on fire, how many ways could be used to reach you? What if you were in a ten-story building?
13. Describe how an archeologist might prepare for a dig. Can you demonstrate this?
14. In your opinion, does the information presented in the exhibit about the beginning of man justify the comparisons between man and ape?
15. Which of these two displays that illustrate the location of discoveries in a dig is the best in showing how bone parts are discovered? Justify your choice.
16. If you discovered what you thought looked like old bones in your backyard, what would you do? Tell us the sequence of events that you would follow.
17. What adaptations do you think that man will have to make in order to survive in the twenty-first century?
18. Observe the train. Now line up like a train and tell us

the car that you would like to have represented on the train. Why did you select that car?

19. Observe the office of the train station master. Infer the jobs that the station master would perform.

20. Compare the old tools observed in the cabinetmaker's shop with those used today. Who can tell us some comparisons?

21. Why don't we observe three-story, twenty-room log cabins?

22. Classify the articles in the log cabin according to shape. Next try material. Why does wood seem to dominate in your classification scheme?

23. Pretend you are living in a log cabin. What would your chores be? Where would you sleep? What would you eat? Where would you go to the restroom?

24. What would have happened if the dinosaurs had not become extinct? How would our lives have been affected?

25. Close your eyes. Using only your senses of smell and sound, what can you tell me about this object?

26. Describe how the animal's fur feels. Does it feel like anything that you are familiar with?

27. What if you were the largest animal living in this cave? How would you live and where would you obtain your food? What if you were the smallest animal?

28. Observe the animals on the merry-go-round. How can you find out if they *really* go up and down?

29. Describe how it feels to ride on a merry-go-round.

30. What would you like to have added to this exhibit and why?

31. What would you like to have eliminated from this exhibit and why?

32. Calculate the number of revolutions that the carousel makes in one minute? One day? One year? (Hint: use a calculator.)

33. Locate the object that you like best and stand in front of it. Why did you choose it?

34. Locate the object that you like least and stand in front of it. Why did you choose it?

35. How can you account for the fact that many fire engines today are no longer red in color? Why did they make them red in the first place?

36. Think of reasons why we don't use steam engines any more for transportation.

37. Why do you think that trains have a caboose at the end?

38. Observe the exhibit, and as I describe certain features, go stand in front of the object being described. How many clues will it take you to discover the object that I am talking about?

39. How is a fire like a rifle? How is a fire different from a rifle?

40. Compare and contrast how the markings on a turtle's shell are like the outside of a rock.

41. If you were an ancient Egyptian, what kinds of gods would you believe in?

42. Suppose you were a cave man. You have just been hunting, and you killed a bear. You brought him into your cave. What do you think would happen next?

43. Observe the teepee. Infer how its shape and structure enable it to be easily moved from place to place.

44. Demonstrate how you would communicate information to another person without either speaking or writing.

45. Observe the exhibit. Who can locate the largest object? The smallest object?

46. What is this exhibit trying to communicate to you?

47. If you could only use *one* word to describe this exhibit, what would it be?

48. Develop your own classification scheme for the museum. What would it be like? Would your scheme have categories, such as things that move or things that are blue?

49. Many of these photographs have windows in them. Why would someone want to have so many photographs with windows in them?

50. How do you explain the order that this person used for hanging these paintings? What does this particular order communicate to you? What changes would you make in this order and why?

51. What do you like about this painting and why?
52. If you were purchasing one of these paintings for yourself, which one would you select and why?
53. How do you feel about using acorns in art?
54. What does this series of pictures tell us about our environment?
55. How would this photograph change if it were taken on a cloudy day?
56. What emotion(s) does this painting evoke in you?
57. If you owned a dress shop, would you hire the person who created the window in this photograph as your window designer? Why or why not?
58. Can you suggest two additional paintings that could be used to complete the exhibition?
59. How many triangles or shades of blue can you locate in this painting?
60. How does this painting relate to the title? What title would you give to this painting? Why?
61. How do you account for the fact that the artist made the birds pink instead of blue?
62. Why do you think that the artist begins and ends the exhibit with a car?
63. Select your photograph. Tell us why you chose it.
64. Observe the painting. Infer the direction from which the light is coming.
65. What features make this painting interesting to you?
66. Which parts of the painting would you like to touch and why? Smell? Taste?
67. Which painting would you like to hear sounds from? Why?
68. How do the different colors in the painting make you feel?
69. What do you think will happen next in the picture?
70. What do you infer the black shape is in this painting?
71. Why do you think that the photographer chose to photograph this man here?
72. Which of these backgrounds would you choose for your portrait and why?

73. Do you think that this painter likes his work? How can you tell?
74. Observe this painting. Identify the items for sale in this store using the clues.
75. How are the horse and the dragonlike animal alike? How are they different?
76. Select the paintings that illustrate happiness. What colors are used to illustrate this?
77. Considering your mood today, which painting uses the colors that best express it? What colors are they?
78. Match the clues on the clue sheet to the painting.
79. Which painting shows your favorite season? Have someone guess what that season is.
80. Which painting illustrates the season of fall? How do you know?
81. Can you locate two paintings that use curved or rounded shapes as a fundamental component? Point them out.
82. What type of material do you infer is inside each of these pillows? Which one would you prefer to sleep on and why?
83. How would you convince someone to trade one of their articles for one of yours?
84. Suppose you wanted to build a model of a trading post. What would you include in your model?
85. Do you think that the trading between the Indian and the French settlers was fair? Justify your answer.
86. Why did early man paint on cave walls? Does modern man paint on cave walls today? Justify your answers.
87. Why do you think that the wearing and collecting of jewelry is valued so much by people?
88. How would you change Tyrannosaurus rex's legs to look like Archaeopteryx's legs?
89. Observe the paintings. What can you tell us about the use of shadows? Make similar shadows for us.
90. What are some things we might do to change the materials so that we could test these ideas?
91. If I were to change this feature, what can we expect to happen?

92. Before I begin this demonstration, what are some of the crucial points that I should think about?
93. What are some other things that you can suggest that might have changed the results?
94. What shapes can you make in the air using just your fingers?
95. Suppose you wanted to design a model of the fastest airplane in the world. What parts, if any, would appear differently on the fastest airplane in the world? How would you describe it to me?
96. Who can use his body to form a circle? A triangle? A square? A rectangle?
97. Look at the object through the cardboard tube. Who can describe what they observe?
98. Now that you have experienced our *collections*, what collections do you and your family have?
99. Describe the object with your eyes closed. How does it feel? What do you infer that it is?
100. How would you feel if you only grew up to be two feet tall? What would the advantages and/or disadvantages be?
101. Listen to the sounds. Which ones are pleasant? Which ones are unpleasant? What makes some sounds pleasant and some unpleasant? Which do you prefer and why?

Before proceeding on to Chapter 3 you can add the next ninety-nine questions to give your guided tour a repertoire of 200 questions for starters! (Divergent, of course.)

Chapter 3

EDUCATIONAL PROGRAMS

A person's mind is not a sponge.
It is more a well-spring.
Alfred DeVito, 1981

"WHAT is that big building over there?"
"That's the museum. Someday I am going to stop in and see what it's like. I was there in the fourth grade and as I remember it, they had some interesting things."

This is a comment that has been made over and over again at almost every museum in the country. Traditionally museums have been considered as something different; a place apart from the ordinary, everyday things of life. A special place; a place you must go to. . . *sometime.*

And museums, until recently, have agreed with this traditional role. They have considered themselves primarily as institutions of *open* education. The museum constituency was thought to want self-education and therefore, the simple display of objects and materials would provide all the stimulus that was needed.

Gradually, over the years, both the museums and the museum public have begun to see themselves in new roles. Museums are increasingly involved in more formal programs of education. The public is beginning to think of museums as not just a place to go and look, but a place to participate.

As with all change, it is not an overnight accomplishment. Not something that everyone thinks is right or even agrees with. Recently a high school class of juniors was asked, *What type of of people visit a museum?* The reasons given the most were that *older people came because they were more interested and could see things they remembered* and *children on class trips or with their families* (in other words *forced* groups). Halfway down the list of reasons was that it was a place to learn; a place that was interesting.

Museums, themselves, are not noted for their tendency toward changes. Many are 100 percent for progress but 99 percent against *untried* changes. They offer many valid reasons for this feeling: *Our staff is too small (or we don't have any staff). . . Our budget won't allow us to experiment (or we don't have any budget). . . It might work in a large institution, but not here. . . Maybe later, but not now. . . We'll ask the board (the committee, the director) about it and see what they say. . .*

All of this reasoning is valid, should be considered, taken into account and then acted upon, worked around or considered as a *creative challenge*. All people, whether adult or child, are generally curious, like to explore and want to learn if properly motivated. It is up to the museum profession to find the best ways to take advantage of these traits.

Educational research shows us that enthusiasm for learning is related to interest. Thus, a person who has a chance to participate in an activity will learn more than a person who just listens or looks. Furthermore, some *fun* or *joy* will help us to get our message across. It is more fun to discover things for ourselves through a learning process than to be told what we should know.

However, it is not easy to give up control of what museum professionals think that the public needs to know. It is not easy to let the public *discover* and *explore* because they may miss the important facts that we know they should have. It requires faith in your knowledge, staff, public, and institution to release that control. But we do want to get our message across, whatever it may be. We do want people to learn. And in some cases we even want to bring about change in attitudes, preconceived ideas, or erroneous information.

So, what do we do? How do we go about getting our message out? How do we communicate our goals to the public? Over the years, museums have tried many different ways. We are now

going to look at some of the more *tried-and-true* methods used —
but look at them perhaps a little differently with an added twist
here and there.

EXHIBITS

Exhibits are the one thing that every museum must have in
some form or another. They range from putting everything we
own on shelves and letting everyone come and view our *open
storage* exhibits to an empty room with a platform where we can
spotlight one item from our collection and let the public *interact*
with it. Some institutions have a whole department that works
on exhibits — researchers, exhibit designers, and a staff to install
and educational personnel to implement. Others have no staff
and no budget — only artifacts, a place to display, and interested
people (often untrained in the art of display) to put the exhibit
together.

Traditionally, museums have been a repository for artifacts, a
place to do research and gain knowledge. The exhibits have been
a distillation of this research and knowledge, open to all, nondi-
dactic, to be taken or left alone as desired. And that is not all
bad, but it can be better. Through exhibits we can focus attention, change ideas, expose people to new information and even
motivate action. But to do this we must reach the person viewing
the exhibit, we must get their attention, we must involve them in
some way. Research shows that the average person touring a museum on his own will glance at an exhibit for about forty-five seconds before moving on unless something catches his attention.
That is not long! Obviously something is needed!

This is not a book on exhibit design, but rather a book on
how we can use an exhibit as a learning tool. Therefore, let it suf-
fice to say that color, design, and presentation of artifacts are important and must be carefully planned and implemented. But we
will concentrate on ways of using the exhibit.

Labeling is an in-between area. One of those *gray areas* that
seem to constantly come up in any well-organized project. Labels
should be short, informative, and easy to read and should pull
the viewer in. One time honored method is to ask questions.
Questions can call for an immediate response, make a person

think, draw a comparison, or create an interest in reading further. Questions work! They can be used effectively in almost any circumstance whether it be labeling, tours, writing; they help to break down the barriers; they involve the participant.

Letting people touch is another way to break down the barriers. This is not always possible because of display cases, security demands, and responsibility of protecting collections. However, with a little thought and additional effort we could provide this opportunity more often than we do. Some artifacts are not really going to be hurt by touching and, if safely displayed, would not need to be in a case. A stone axe could be touched innumerable times without showing any ill effects. Projectile points mounted on a wall could be both seen and felt. A spinning wheel could be used during a special exhibit.

Sometimes the actual object might not be available to touch, but a reproduction or similiar material would still add a new dimension. A piece of marble, both raw and finished, might add to the appreciation of a statue. A piece of fur next to the polar bear would satisfy the question, *Is it as soft as it looks?*

The removal of visual barriers can give the visitor the impression that he could touch if he wanted to, even when it is not really possible. Sometimes, just the feeling of *availability* is enough to satisfy the viewer.

In recent years the use of media devices (recordings, film, light shows) have been much in evidence in museums. They add a whole new dimension to interpretation. The sound of the carousel or the noise of the political rally, make it much easier to involve yourself in an experience. Films can create the time period of an artifact, set the stage for what is going to happen, explain a complicated premise, and provide the visitor with needed information. A computer questioning device or even a light board with questions and answers act as an *attention getter* for both children and adults. But this equipment is often expensive to produce, install, and keep in working order. Many institutions do not have the staff or budget to make its use possible. However, a tape recording could be used for special events, a flip-card board can serve the same purpose as the electronic device, and illustrations, traced with the help of an opaque projector, can add to the exhibit. They may not be quite as effective as the more sophisticated devices, but they do help to get the message across.

UNGUIDED VISITORS

Printed materials also will add to exhibit interpretation, if you can encourage people to read them. Many institutions have catalogs that provide additional information about exhibits. These can range from mimeographed pickup sheets to professionally done slick-covered publications complete with pictures and/or illustrations. Sometimes they are free, sometimes for purchase; but all need to be obtained to be used. The viewer has to be interested enough to pick them up or purchase them — they demand an interested audience before they can be effective.

Suggestion sheets can be available for unguided visitors. Often family groups will come to the museum and the parents want to provide an interesting experience for their children. They will essentially act as the docent for their children — they want or need to be the expert; but they do not know the territory. Some form of suggestion sheet such as shown in Figure 3-1 could be useful. This will help both the adult and the child as they visit the museum since many visitors do not know how to observe or read an artifact. A search game can help both the parent and the child to focus their attention and have an objective for their museum visit. If an institution is large, the theme sequence format, as shown in Figure 3-2, can be helpful.

DOCENT-LED TOURS

Suggestions thus far have been for your casual, unguided visitor. Now let us look at your guided or toured visitors. According to Shirley Low, supervisor of Hostess Training at Colonial Williamsburg: *The best type of interpretation for any historic site is one given in person by a well-informed, enthusiastic and friendly human being.*[1]

This quote can apply to any kind of instutition from an art gallery to a zoo. But, of course there are problems that must be solved. The questions of budget and personnel have to be answered. Where will you obtain docents? Who will pay for them? Will they be volunteers? Who will train them? How will you recruit docents? How many can you obtain? Will all visitors be guided?

---

[1]Shirley P. Low, "Historic Site Interpretation: The Human Approach," *History News*, November, 1965, p. 2.

We all know how to read a book, a letter or even instructions—but how do you read an artifact (object)?

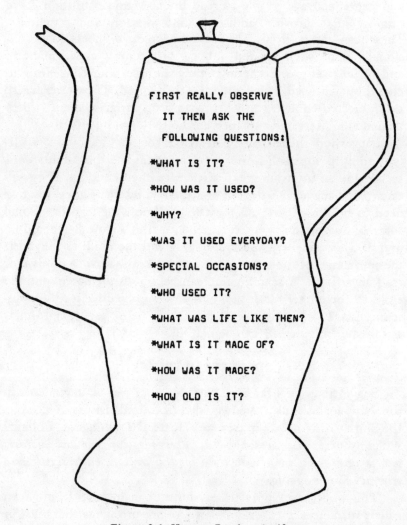

FIRST REALLY OBSERVE
IT THEN ASK THE
FOLLOWING QUESTIONS:

*WHAT IS IT?

*HOW WAS IT USED?

*WHY?

*WAS IT USED EVERYDAY?

*SPECIAL OCCASIONS?

*WHO USED IT?

*WHAT WAS LIFE LIKE THEN?

*WHAT IS IT MADE OF?

*HOW WAS IT MADE?

*HOW OLD IS IT?

Figure 3-1. How to *Read* an Artifact

Will only special groups be guided? Where will you get the groups? The list seems to go on and on. Then you need to remember the words *well-informed, enthusiastic, and friendly human being.* Nothing can turn a visitor off faster than a bored or uninformed docent who will not allow a visitor the chance to fol-

Welcome to the Museum! Today while you are here why
don't you play our <u>On the Move</u>! game. See how many ways you
can find that people have used to get from one place to another.

Figure 3-2. On the Move!

low his own interests.

Potential docents may be found in the most unexpected
places:

— other community organizations
— parents on field trips

— through advertising: in your newsletter, library bulletin
boards, local media
— special interest groups
— a blank on your membership form

Once you have found docents, you will of course want to set
up your own training program. This program will stress your own
institution's goals and objectives. Training might include knowledge to be transmitted, forms of interpretation, educational
techniques, methodology, and philosophy.

The rest of the problems mentioned must be solved, depending on the requirements of your own situation. So let us assume
that all of these problems have now been resolved and explore
the advantages of docent-led tours.

First, they make achieving your museum's objectives much
easier since you have direct contact with the visitor. They provide a security factor and perhaps most importantly they give
your visitors someone to interact with. On a docent-led tour you
can use handling materials, work demonstrations into a tour, direct attention to important points, and answer questions imme-
diately. With role playing and costuming, another time period or
different location can be recreated. It is well and good to say you
can do these things. But how do you actually go about it?

PREVISIT MATERIALS

Previsit materials may be sent to a group ahead of time so
that they will have some idea what to expect when they arrive.
These can range from the very factual — such as time, place to
meet the docent, or name tags, to providing an introductory experience before they even get to the museum. Figure 3-3 illustrates an example of an informational sheet that can be enclosed
along with school tour confirmation forms. You can revise this
model to fit the unique information for your museum.

The informational sheet shown in Figure 3-4 provides an opportunity to prepare groups for the visit. It also gives the docent
a starting point with which to build rapport when the group arrives at the museum.

Dear Teacher:

This checklist is for you to use with your class before your trip to the _____ Museum, please feel free to copy it as needed.

We would like your class to realize that:

1. A museum can be in any kind of building--this museum happens to be a _____.

2. A museum is similar to a library in that it is a place to learn about things--either from actually observing the object or using the research library and archives.

3. While a museum is <u>not</u> a place to run and yell; it is also <u>not</u> a place that you have to be very quiet and not ask questions. We would like your class to be controlled, but still their usual responsive selves.

4. Historical societies and museums have four main purposes:

   a. <u>collecting</u> artifacts, documents and other data relative to the history of a particular area.

   b. <u>preserving</u> these items for future generations

   c. <u>researching</u> these items in order to gain as much understanding from them as possible

   d. <u>interpreting</u> these items and the results of the research to the public

5. In line with the above purposes there will be some objects that can only be looked at and not touched; however, there are also objects that they will be able to listen to, touch, and handle.

We hope that your students will discover that a museum is not a scary, old and dusty place--but a place where they can enjoy themselves and learn. We are looking forward to having your class visit us!

                                        Sincerely,

Figure 3-3.

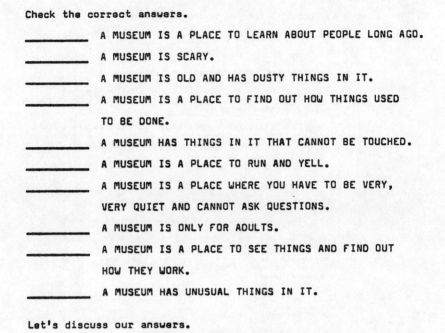

Check the correct answers.

_____ A MUSEUM IS A PLACE TO LEARN ABOUT PEOPLE LONG AGO.

_____ A MUSEUM IS SCARY.

_____ A MUSEUM IS OLD AND HAS DUSTY THINGS IN IT.

_____ A MUSEUM IS A PLACE TO FIND OUT HOW THINGS USED

TO BE DONE.

_____ A MUSEUM HAS THINGS IN IT THAT CANNOT BE TOUCHED.

_____ A MUSEUM IS A PLACE TO RUN AND YELL.

_____ A MUSEUM IS A PLACE WHERE YOU HAVE TO BE VERY,

VERY QUIET AND CANNOT ASK QUESTIONS.

_____ A MUSEUM IS ONLY FOR ADULTS.

_____ A MUSEUM IS A PLACE TO SEE THINGS AND FIND OUT

HOW THEY WORK.

_____ A MUSEUM HAS UNUSUAL THINGS IN IT.

Let's discuss our answers.

Figure 3-4. What is a Museum?

Previsit materials can also be sent to the school or group ahead of time to prepare for a specific tour activity when they come to the museum. For example, the pioneer tour could include a session in a pioneer school. Information sent to the group ahead of time could include the following:

— Rationale:

This activity is designed to let the students draw their own conclusions after exploring a variety of historical information and then to test their conclusions in a role playing situation.

— Objectives for Activity:

To give the group a chance to compare their school to a pioneer school.

To allow the group to draw their own conclusions about why a pioneer school was different from their school today.

To allow the group to gain new perspectives about the role of education.

— Materials:

Various pioneer period school artifacts: slate, quill, ink recipe, school bell, reproductions of sample textbooks

Data sheets about the pioneer school including: number and ages of students, background of community, background of teacher, working conditions of the time. (This should include copies of letters, maps, and other documents.)

When the group visits the museum the docent will give them additional material relative to the local pioneer period and then involve the class in a school role playing situation. Since the group has already studied the composition and the life-style of the community through their previsit activities, the docent is able to provide in-depth interpretation of the pioneer period using artifacts in the museum exhibit.

GAMES AND SEARCHES

There are many activities that will add to docent-led tours without advance preparation. These activities are designed to —

— Focus visitors' attention on an exhibit
— Help visitors compare and/or contrast
— Give visitors a chance to verbalize and interact
— Provide opportunities for involvement
— Provide information for discussion

For younger visitors, a *Treasure Hunt* type of activity will accomplish these objectives. Let them work individually or in groups, making sure that the rules are clear and that some type of incentive or reward is provided.

Questions that make the students think are better than single answer type questions. During the discussion at the conclusion of the tour a thinking exercise can also be utilized.

Example 1: Search question: *What is a fleam?*

Answer: "A fleam is a surgical instrument used to cut a blood vessel."

Discussion: "Why would they need a surgical instrument like that?"

"What would you do with a surgical instrument like a fleam?"

Example 2: Search question: *What season does this exhibit*
                                   show?

              Answer: "Fall."

              Discussion: "How can you tell this is a Fall
                            scene?"
                            "What can you observe that indi-
                            cates that this exhibit is about
                            Fall?"

Figure 3-5.

The *Treasure Hunt* approach does not have to be limited to factual answers. You can ask *abstract* or *feeling* questions and use the answers to lead into interesting discussions. Find something that makes you feel happy or sad or that looks hard or soft or warm or cold, then you can discuss why it makes them feel that way. Was the object designed to make you feel that way? Would you be comfortable sitting on that hard chair? What were the reasons that it was made that way?

Figure 3-5 illustrates pictures that may be substituted for written communication.

ACTIVITY CARDS

Activity cards are another good way to encourage people to think and become involved. Prepare a series of cards and pass them out to groups of three or four visitors. Let these groups work on their project and then have them bring the results back to share through a group discussion. This is a good way for the visitors to relate what they are familiar with to what they are observing or to draw inferences from knowledge that they already possess.

Several examples:

1. In what way(s) is this fireplace like the stove in your kitchen? How is it different?
2. In what way(s) is a beaver like a buffalo? How is it different?
3. If the gasoline engine had been invented by 1700, how would this exhibit have been changed?

Another way to approach the exhibit, either verbally or with cards, is to ask what has just happened before the exhibit. *The dinosaur has just knocked over the tree. The steamboat has just docked. The teacher has just rung the school bell.* You can also ask what will happen right after the event depicted. *They will win/lose the battle and _____ will happen. The hawk will catch the rabbit. The glass blower will attach a handle to his pitcher.*

DATA RETRIEVAL SHEETS

A data retrieval sheet is a particularly useful tool to use with older visitors. It is very adaptable and will help focus a group's attention on the object desired. A data retrieval sheet will —
- Help concentrate the visitor's attention while exploring museum exhibits
- Provide visitors information to use at the conclusion of the tour for discussion
- Stimulate interaction and discussion that will lead to additional activities
- Help visitors compare and/or contrast

An example of a data retrieval sheet is shown in Figure 3-6.

	As seen in the following exhibits:			
Focus	Woodland Indian	Pioneer	Transportation	Victorian Parlor
Role of Women				
Role of Men				
Life-style: Economy				
Role of Children				
Role of Elders				

Figure 3-6. Data Retrieval Sheet

Data retrieval sheets can also be used to gather data for interdisciplinary projects related to the areas of mathematics, science, English, art, history, etc. This is an excellent way for a high school age visitor to do research, draw conclusions, compile statistics, and prepare reports. Museums offer a wide variety of opportunities for these activities through the decorative arts, architecture, application of inventions, settlement patterns, etc.

GUIDED VISIT THEMES

Visiting the museum can be an overwhelming and fragmented experience; a kaleidoscope of sensations and information that all too often results in fatigue and bewilderment for the visitor. The focused guided visit structured around a particular theme or concept helps the visitor to organize the exhibit information into a meaningful whole. Each visited exhibit reflects and reiterates the same unifying idea.

The guided visit topic may be directly linked to a school curriculum. For example, the guided visit *Home Sweet Home* might focus upon man's varied and often ingenious efforts to provide shelter for himself and his family and stresses the importance of influence of environment and life-style on man's creation of a house. The visit might include observing the African, Native American, Eskimo, and Americana shelter exhibits. *Home Sweet Home* could fulfill the local school system's primary grade curriculum objective: to help student's understand how a people's need for shelter is satisfied by using a comparative, cultural, anthropological approach.

Guided visits may be organized around an idea that introduces the teacher's goal of initiating his class to the museum experience. The guided visit *Exploring the Children's Museum* is an experience that could provide the students with an opportunity to acquaint themselves with some of the numerous and varied exhibits at the museum. Structured for grades kindergarten through eighth grade the students could visit the following exhibits: a cave, live animals, dinosaurs, mummies, Native Americans, toys and dolls, and toy trains.

The thematic approach allows one to look to the broader underlying messages of the exhibits. The theme serves as a unifying device, which focuses the visitors' observations. The guided visit is organized around selected exhibits that reflect themes. This approach encourages the use of essentially static and unchanging exhibits in new and varied ways. It directs the attention of the group and emphasizes a particular concept or idea. It also allows the docent to develop activities that relate to themes. Such an approach alleviates the visitor's mad dash through the museum. Instead the group visits only those exhibits that relate to themes.

The development of student skills, refinement of attitudes, and the acquisition of knowledge are important educational goals for schools. Guided visits can successfully integrate these goals into the thematic approach. *Searching for Shapes* is another example of a guided visit which incorporates the primary grades classroom skill-building work of recognizing and matching shapes. The visit's objective is to concentrate the child's attention upon museum objects and exhibits by identifying the predominant shape or shapes as they appear in those objects. The docent's role is to help the students observe the form of the triangle in the tipi, the forms of the rectangle and circle in the Eskimo parka, and the various shapes as they appear in a fish or turtle and to consider how the shape influences function, movement, and efficiency. The objective of the guided visit is to help the student move from the specific to the general.

In summary, the thematic organization helps the teacher select relevant museum experiences for his class. The guided visit can be selected in conjunction with specific teaching objectives and classroom studies. It also encourages the teacher to view the guided visit as an extension of the classroom learning and encourages the development of premuseum and postmuseum visit activities establishing bridges of continuity between the classroom and the museum.

PROBLEM-SOLVING ACTIVITIES

A problem is a situation, either quantitative or qualitative, that is used to confront an individual or group of individuals for resolution. The individual sees no obvious means or path for obtaining the solution. In order to be a problem worthy of consideration, three criteria must be satisfied: the individual must accept the confrontation as a problem; the initial attempts at solution are fruitless, that is, normal responses and patterns of attack do not work; and the problem acceptance results in new methods of attack to solve the problem.

A problem is *not* considered a problem if it can be easily solved as a result of previous learning. Most *story problems* are not really problems at all, but are based upon some model solution. Few of these types of so-called problems foster higher level thinking, and many of these are boring to both children and adults.

Problem solving is a process. It is the means by which an individual uses previously acquired knowledge, skills, and understanding to respond to an unfamiliar situation. There are twelve ways that docents can encourage children and adults to become successful problem solvers:

1. An atmosphere for success must be created by the docent.
2. Visitors must be encouraged to solve problems.
3. Visitors should be physically involved in the problem solving process through the use of manipulative materials.
4. Visitors should be encouraged to create their own problems.
5. Visitors should be encouraged to discuss problems with each other.
6. Visitors should be encouraged to use drawings to illustrate the problem being considered.
7. Alternative approaches should be suggested when the existing approach appears to have reached a dead end.
8. Docents need to raise creative, constructive questions, and they need to remember that problem solving takes *time*. Time to think and time to respond.
9. Creativity of thought and imagination needs to be emphasized.
10. Docents should encourage the purchase and use of calculators and microcomputers for problem solving.
11. Docents should use strategy problem solving games to help sharpen problem solving skills.
12. Docents should not overly emphasize the mathematical concepts that may be involved in problem solving.

Sample problem solving activities that could be used for motivational purposes are listed below:

— How many times can you bounce this rubber ball in one minute? What variables must be taken into account when solving this problem? What if we changed the size of the ball? The shape? The weight?

— One hamburger franchise has sold more than 22 billion hamburgers, each of which is 2.5 centimetres thick. If we stacked these hamburgers on top of one another, how many kilometres high would the stack be?

— How many different ways can three people divide twenty-five pieces of candy so that each person receives at least one piece? Develop the equation to solve this problem. (Using twenty-five actual pieces of candy helps to solve this problem.) The answer is 276 ways; how did we arrive at that answer?

— Design and demonstrate a glass that will not spill.

— On traffic lights, which color is on top? Why do you think they put this color on top? Design a better traffic light.

— How many ways can you empty a glass of water that is sitting on a table without touching either the glass or the table?

— Using six toothpicks, make four triangles that all have the same length sides.

— List all of the foods that you can think of that are green.

— List all of the ice cream flavors that you can think of.

— List all of the uses that could be made from an empty plastic butter container.

Additional information for problem solving along with sample problems can be found in the references listed in the Bibliography.

TACTILE EXPERIENCES

It is an accepted contemporary view that the optimum learning experience is one in which the visitor is an active participant. All visitors respond positively to situations that allow them the opportunity for touching, but for some visitors, touching is an essential part of the learning process. The museum's role as a con-

servator of material culture is often at odds with its commitment
to the visitor's education. However, if the museum is to successfully fulfill its educational goal it must provide tactile experiences for its visitors, especially for children and disabled persons.

Children learn largely by active involvement, with emphasis
upon sensory experiences. Seeing, hearing, touching, and smelling
are for the child concrete experiences that form the basis for abstract thinking. Children must initially move from the concrete
and literal to the abstract in the development of thought. Many
times children are unable to discern the material that museum
specimens are made from. The exhibit distances the child from
the specimen and establishes a barrier, which prevents the child
from physically exploring it. So while the child can distinguish
between hardness and softness, wooden carousel horses are often
perceived as made from iron and baskets are considered a form of
plastic. The child's perception is based upon his personal experiences and the relationships he draws between them and his museum experiences. The museum object can be perceived and interpreted by the child only in light of his prior experiences.

Disabled visitors must also be given the chance to engage all
their senses in physical exploration, and museum objects can provide multisensory involvements. Hands-on experiences with objects have proven to be most effective for teaching the disabled.
Much importance must be placed on texture, size, smell, and
sound, which together form the totality of the object and aid
the disabled person in their interpretation. The disabled person
must touch to understand.

How then can the museum meet the sensory needs of its visitors? The establishment of a nucleus of touchables is one way to
accomplish this. Touchables are specimens that the museum
views as expendable and hence can be made available to the visitor for handling. Expendable material may be purchased specifically for handling purposes; it may be considered too inferior in
quality for exhibition; it may be reproduced or undocumented.
Any of these things diminish the material's traditional value for
the collections and allow the museum to make the items accessible to the visitor for handling and exploring.

Touchable specimens may be used as an integral part of the guided visit or utilized informally in an exhibit gallery for non-guided visitors. When selecting touchables for a guided visit the docent must consider the focus of the guided visit, the objectives to be accomplished, the exhibit areas to be visited, and the age and interests of the group. For example, a guided visit entitled *Girls and Boys/Men and Women* examines the roles that males and females played in the traditional native American and Eskimo cultures. One objective is to show how the adult roles of men and women are mirrored in their activities as boys and girls. With the theme and objective in mind the docent might choose a spear-the-fish game, an ulu, arrowhead, scraper, or a doll for handling material. This material provides not only tactile experiences for the guided group, but also allows the docent to question, explain, and elaborate as he responds to the group. The docent may select some touchables, discuss each object with the group, respond to their questions, and while the group remains seated, pass the objects among them. Or after discussing the objects with the group, he may place them on a cart, allowing the group, to independently explore both the exhibit gallery and tactile material at will.

Handling material can also be used with the random visitor. The docent selects handling material that complements a particular exhibit and, placing the material on a table or cart, invites museum visitors to freely explore objects and to ask questions about them. The touchables should appeal to a broad age range and reflect the concepts and information presented in the exhibit. The docent responds to visitor questions, explains how the material relates to the exhibit, and informally engages the visitor in discussions about the objects.

To effectively use the materials the docent must be familiar with how the objects were used, know the material or materials from which they are derived, understand the object's significance to both the culture with which it is linked and our culture, and be familiar with the cultural group and period with which the article is identified. For it is only when the docent is comfortable with the material that he can engage the visitor in a dialogue concerning it.

Tactile kits look not to the object but to the material from which the object is formed to stimulate learning and understanding. Too often visitors are engaged in discussions about museum objects without understanding how the object evolved. In some instances, if one is unable to visualize the raw material that forms the object, one cannot appreciate or understand the concepts or ideas implied by the object. For example, this is especially true of the material culture found in a native American exhibit gallery. Much importance is placed upon the native American's inventiveness and his understanding and use of nature to survive, but if one has never experienced untanned deerskin, touched buffalo skin, or known what birchbark is, it becomes impossible to successfully integrate what the docent is revealing about deerskin clothing, buffalo tipis, and birchbark containers and canoes into learning. Certainly, the significance of the docent's remarks are diminished.

A native American tactile kit requires only bits and pieces of deer, fox, buffalo, rabbit fur, a few beads, porcupine quills, birchbark, and grass specimens. The material can be stored in shoe boxes, wooden carrying cases, or drawers.

One of the more effective ways of utilizing the kits is for the docent to involve the guided group in a gallery search. Each person is given a tactile item and told to explore the exhibit area in search of an object made from the material. They must report back to the group and be able to identify their tactile item, have located an object in the exhibit created from it, explain how the object was used, and tell how it might have been important to the cultural group. The tactile search encourages an exploration of the exhibits while helping the visitor to more closely observe the exhibit objects.

SIMULATION ACTIVITIES

Simulation or representation activities can be an excellent method for relating *real life* experiences to visitors.

One excellent example of a simulation activity that relates the experiences of an archeologist who unearths a civilization of the past and the resulting explanations can be found in the book

Motel of the Mysteries by David Macaulay, Houghton Mifflin Company, 2 Park Street, Boston, MA 02107, 1979.

Motel of the Mysteries relates the discoveries of an archeologist who has found the buried ruins of a twentieth Century motel in the year 4022. Some of the *artifacts* found in Tomb 26 (Room 26) included the following:

Interpretation	Actuality
The great altar	Television set
Ceremonial platform	Bed
Ceremonial head dress	Shower cap
White sarcophagus	Bathtub
Music box	Toilet tank
Sacred seal	Do not disturb sign

The descriptions can be presented and then the visitors should attempt to identify the object being described. This method will also work well with any museum artifact in order to encourage visitors to visualize and describe artifacts. Furthermore, visitors can speculate as to the use of these artifacts, keeping in mind that the interpretation regarding the use of artifacts is subject to modification as new evidence becomes available.

Simulations that involve the use of one's imagination are also useful for involving visitors. One example might be the following:

Imagine that you are a television interviewer. A variety of people come to your program to be interviewed. You want to learn as much as possible about each person but you only have time to ask each person three questions. What three questions would you ask each of these people?

— A pioneer living in 1781.
— An Egyptian slave building a pyramid.
— A docent who was just selected Docent of the Year.
— An astronaut.
— A train conductor.

Simulation of an event can also serve to involve visitors. Simulations such as a reenactment of an historic event or natural castastrophe can also serve to relate events of importance to the visitor of today.

Another aspect to the use of simulations is the use of models. Docents can utilize models to help visitors develop a clearer understanding of the material being presented. Models can be used to represent *real things*, such as a model of an airplane (either the same size or scaled to size). A model can also be a representation of something that we cannot actually observe such as the model of our universe or the model of an atom. And finally, models can be based upon the representation of data such as a mathematical model for population that could be graphed.

Next time you use the vending machine at the museum to obtain a candy bar, you can begin to build your own model. Observe the vending machine and write a description of what you believe happens *inside* the machine to deliver a candy bar to you after you insert the coin. The observations that you have collected are that you put a coin in one slot and candy comes out of a different opening in the machine. The explanation that you have just written is your model of what the inside of the machine looks like and what goes on in it to deliver the candy to you. It is likely that your model and the actual working parts of the machine do not closely resemble each other. This is not really very important as long as the model that you have constructed supports the evidence you have and as long as that support stands the test of time. Model building is one very important aspect of museum education because it permits visitors to relate their present observations to their previous experiences with similar systems, such as the model of a fort, pyramid, or Egyptian tomb. Models also satisfy the need for thinking in concrete terms. They also lead to predictions and to new discoveries about the object or exhibit being investigated.

Model simulations that have been successfully used by docents include the following:
— The space shuttle
— The Battle of Bunker Hill
— An automobile assembly line
— The flat world of Ancient Greece
— The Declaration of Independence
— The first settlement in New England in 1607

Now you are ready to develop some model simulations of your own to use with your visitors.

ROLE PLAYING AND COSTUMING

The idea of docents wearing costumes is sometimes confused with role playing. Both forms of interpretation have much to offer docent-led tours.

Costuming can be beneficial to your program. The costumes must be authentic enough in style and fabric to give an accurate impression of the period you want to represent. Either staff or volunteers can research a period and find appropriate styles, colors, and fabrics that can reproduce the desired costumes in available materials. Depending on your budget and the attitude of your docents, the costumes can then either be made by the institution or the docents. The *putting on* of a costume can offer a definite psychological boost to your docents. It can help them to mentally remove themselves from their everyday personality and become the *tour leader*. Some people have expressed the feeling that once they are in costume they feel more outgoing and confident — almost a *stage* presence. Costuming also has the advantage of making your docents very visible. On a large site it has the advantage of making the docents stand out. It also gives a sense of being someone to listen to before they ever take charge of the tour group. When the docent is in costume, it provides a new depth to interpretation and can help to create a mood for the upcoming tour. It provides the docent with a starting point for their tour; a chance to build rapport with the group before the tour activities actually begin. On the negative side, having costumed docents makes some people feel very uncomfortable and some consider it to be a barrier between them and their tour group. Costuming may not be appropriate in all situations. Some institutions may feel that the impact costuming provides is not worth the necessary time and expense.

Costuming docents may be considered the first step toward a role playing situation. If a role playing situation is to be effective, the person must be costumed. But, this is only a small part of the role playing situation. Role playing requires a great deal of research to provide the necessary information in order to create the role. The entire time period must be researched — life-style, transportation, economic conditions, physical considerations, political influences, etc. Then all of this information must be ap-

plied to the specific circumstances that you are going to represent. After the role has been created, and it could be either a
composite role or an actual historic person, you may then need
to recreate the actual physical surroundings necessary.

Even though the time and monies invested to create a role
playing situation may be great, the rewards may be even greater.
Role playing allows you to recreate another time and/or place for
your visitors. It allows them the chance to participate in an experience that cannot be gained in their everyday lives. For a little
while the visitor can actually observe and experience what it
would be like in another time period, at an historical event, or in
a place they will perhaps never have a chance to visit in actuality
— how it would be to travel in space, what it was like to build a
home in the wilderness. Role playing allows the institution to
present a vast amount of information in an interesting and challenging way to a visitor. It allows the visitors a chance to use all
of their senses and imagination in sharing this experience.

Role playing as a form of interpretation also presents some
other problems that must be solved. Many times the visitors want
to relate their role playing experiences to their present lives. You
must decide whether you will allow your characters to step out
of their roles to answer these questions? How can you explain
events that took place after your role playing situation? For example, what effect did this event have upon the development of
the country, what happened to this person during the next twen-
ty years, or why was this event significant?

You also have to take visitor knowledge and historical accuracy into account. Role playing an historical character may present problems that role playing a composite character would not.
Your visitor may have knowledge that is inaccurate about the
character — how will you deal with this situation? Or perhaps the
true historical picture does not agree with the preconceived public image. The public may not really want to know that Christ-
mas was not a big celebration in the Midwest in the 1830s or that
the pilgrims did not all wear *Pilgrim costumes*. Accurate role
playing is challenging, time consuming, and often expensive, but
it presents unique opportunities.

Many institutions have worked out a compromise solution. A
character or role is developed, then using costuming and minimal

props, this role is worked into the total interpretation. It becomes a *cameo presentation* during the tour. This allows the tour to interact with a person from the period, but holds down research and expenses and solves the problems of answering questions and explaining effect.

POSTVISIT MATERIALS

Follow-up activities are an important part of any learning experience. Postvisit materials and projects can be developed to help the visitors carry the visit beyond the museum. Individual activities, such as word searches or crossword puzzles, are something the visitors enjoy. These type of activities will act as reinforcement for the information gained during the tour and serve to focus the visitor's attention. Since it has the appearance of a game the visitor does not regard it as a *test* of what he has learned, but a *fun* activity.

To create a word-search puzzle you need to identify the questions that emphasize the curriculum requirements, write the answers in the figure and then fill in all blank spaces with additional letters as shown in the example in Figure 3-7. Answers are given in Figure 3-8.

If your budget will not allow you to send copies with each individual on your tours, an alternative is to send one copy with each group. Thus, groups can return to their school or other institution to make the material available for each visitor.

A list of suggested follow-up activities may be all the stimulus that a visitor needs to start all types of projects after the visit. It can provide a course of action or become the starting point for the visitor to fit the museum visit into his future plans. It may even suggest new tours or directions that will lead to another visit. Figure 3-9 provides a sample of suggested activities.

ADDITIONAL ACTIVITIES

We have been discussing methods and activities to use with the visitors that come to your museum. Many people cannot come to your site; therefore, you may want to develop an outreach program. This will make your materials and services available to those that may not be able to use them on site. The

DIRECTIONS: All the answers to the questions below are
hidden in the word-search. Circle the correct
answers. Answers may be vertical, horizontal,
backwards, or at an angle.

```
L  I  N  S  E  Y  W  O  O  L  S  E  Y  P
A  Y  S  L  A  T  E  S  P  F  X  D  G  O
Z  S  B  R  E  H  M  R  T  L  N  P  Y  W
E  L  Y  O  W  O  O  L  C  A  R  D  S  D
D  E  I  U  B  P  L  Y  H  X  A  O  P  E
N  E  X  O  H  G  I  E  U  P  C  O  F  R
U  H  Q  E  W  O  A  R  R  M  O  W  U  H
O  W  T  R  A  P  P  I  N  G  D  E  L  O
R  G  H  O  B  J  V  F  B  I  B  L  E  R
G  N  A  B  E  T  T  Y  L  A  M  P  S  N
E  I  N  G  P  R  W  P  K  F  S  T  U  Q
L  N  S  E  L  G  N  I  H  S  D  O  O  W
T  N  D  B  L  A  C  K  S  M  I  T  H  G
T  I  Q  M  E  Y  W  A  L  K  I  N  G  O
A  P  W  Z  B  P  T  E  L  R  E  V  O  C
B  S  F  C  X  R  N  C  A  N  A  M  L  A
```

1. One of the ways used by pioneers to get food

2. Used in preparing wool to be spun

3. Used to carry the powder for long rifles

4. Was used to make butter

5. Many of the pioneer bowls, dishes, and eating utensils
   were made from this

6. Pioneers used left over grease in this to light their
   cabins

7. The man who made the iron utensils was called _____.

8. Pioneer cooking was done over a _____.

9. These animals were often used to pull the covered
   wagons.

Figure 3-7. Pioneer Word-Search Puzzle

Figure 3-7. (continued)

10. Shaped logs were used to build this shelter.

11. The roof of a pioneer home was usually made from these.

12. This crop was grown to be spun into linen.

13. This material was a combination of wool and linen and was very strong material.

14. This simple machine was used to make thread.

15. Most pioneers reached the area they were settling in by _____.

16. Pupils used these instead of paper to practice their lessons.

17. The two books most often used in pioneer schools were the _____ and the _____.

18. Many pioneers had to take care of their own doctoring--to help with this they often planted _____.

19. The leader of the Indian forces at the Battle of Tippecanoe.

20. The Battle of Tippecanoe was fought near the town of _____.

21. A woven cover that was used on the bed.

22. Teachers used this to call their students to class.

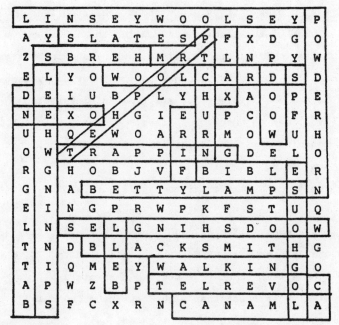

L	I	N	S	E	Y	W	O	O	L	S	E	Y	P
A	Y	S	L	A	T	E	S	P	F	X	D	G	O
Z	S	B	R	E	H	M	R	T	L	N	P	Y	W
E	L	Y	O	W	O	O	L	C	A	R	D	S	D
D	E	I	U	B	P	L	Y	H	X	A	O	P	E
N	E	X	O	H	G	I	E	U	P	C	O	F	R
U	H	Q	E	W	O	A	R	R	M	O	W	U	H
O	W	T	R	A	P	P	I	N	G	D	E	L	O
R	G	H	O	B	J	V	F	B	I	B	L	E	R
G	N	A	B	E	T	T	Y	L	A	M	P	S	N
E	I	N	G	P	R	W	P	K	F	S	T	U	Q
L	N	S	E	L	G	N	I	H	S	D	O	O	W
T	N	D	B	L	A	C	K	S	M	I	T	H	G
T	I	Q	M	E	Y	W	A	L	K	I	N	G	O
A	P	W	Z	B	P	T	E	L	R	E	V	O	C
B	S	F	C	X	R	N	C	A	N	A	M	L	A

1. Trapping	12. Flax
2. Wool cards	13. Linsey-woolsey
3. Powderhorn	14. Spinning wheel
4. Churn	15. Walking
5. Wood	16. Slates
6. Betty lamps	17. Almanac and Bible
7. Blacksmith	18. Herbs
8. Fire	19. Prophet
9. Oxen	20. Battle Ground
10. Log house	21. Coverlet
11. Wood shingles	22. Bell

Figure 3-8. Answers to Pioneer Word-Search Puzzle

1. Keep a make-believe diary about your experience while
   living at the trading post during the 1700s.

2. Write an imaginary letter to your friend in Montreal
   telling about your journey to the interior by canoe.

3. Search your library for all types of information
   available on Woodland Indians. List all of the books,
   magazine articles, filmstrips, pictures, etc. that are
   available.

4. Construct a shoebox diarama to illustrate how you think
   the trading post might have looked.

5. Dress paper dolls as people who might have lived at
   the trading post—French, voyageur, Indian. Give a two
   minute talk about your dressed character.

6. Make an artifact that might have been found in an
   archeological dig at the trading post. Explain how it
   was found and what it was used for.

7. Write a song that the voyageurs might have sung while
   paddling to the trading post. Teach it to some of your
   friends and make a tape-recording.

8. Make a poster advertising the most interesting thing you
   learned on your tour. Display the poster and give a
   two minute talk explaining why you found it interesting.

9. Make a movie about your trip or the history of the
   trading post by drawing a series of pictures on a long
   sheet of paper fastened to two rollers. Write a script
   to go with your movie and present it to your friends.

10. Pantomime some information that you found particularily
    interesting. Let your friends try to guess what you
    are pantomiming.

Figure 3-9. Suggested Activities After a Field Trip to a 1700s' Trading Post

Figure 3-9. (continued)

11. Construct puppets and put on a show about something interesting that you learned about life in the 1700s.

12. Pretend that you are a person living at the trading post (French, Indian, or voyageur) and have a friend interview you as that person. Tape the interview so others may listen.

13. Make up a crossword puzzle about your trading post tour and let other students try to complete it. Check and return their answers.

14. Make up a game that uses information from your tour (for instance a board game about the canoe trip from Montreal with all its hazards). Let other members of your group play the game.

15. Fix up an archeological dig with a box of sand and show what people might learn about your life 200 years later.

reasons for providing such a service would be to —
- Increase the audience you are serving.
- Provide institutions with materials that would not other- wise be available to them.
- Provide a worthwhile educational experience for students in your area that the teacher cannot provide because of lack of knowlege, time, or financial resources.

EDUCATIONAL OR MULTIMEDIA KITS

Educational kits can be developed on almost any subject and include a variety of materials to use in a classroom. Articles in such a kit might include the following:
- Study prints
- Slide show or filmstrip
- Objects
- Models
- Suggested activities

An educational kit can provide the user with a complete package for his use. All that is necessary for the user to do is to schedule the kit, preview it, and follow the instructions. A user would not have to have prior knowledge of a subject, provide ad- ditional materials, or take additional training to obtain a worth- while experience for their constituency.

ACTIVITY KITS

Sometimes persons do not need an entire unit but desire an activity to supplement a unit that is already in progress. For ex- ample, they are studying the Indian history of the area and would like to plan an archeological dig. A kit that includes a film- strip about archeology, some objects to be used in the dig, and the physical materials for the dig would be sufficient. Or, the group has been studying early settlement of the area and would like to concentrate on immigration patterns. Census records, city directories, and newspapers have been used to collect informa- tion. Now they are planning a trip to the cemetery to check their findings. A kit of activities to be used while there would be useful.

CIRCULATING MATERIALS

Often the person just needs some supplemental or handling materials to add depth to his program. A slide show that brings his unit on transportation down to the local level might be the needed culminating activity. Wool cards, fleece, or drop spindles could add interest to a pioneer unit. Art study prints could show various techniques for working with oil paints. This type of material only needs to be made available and safely transported; it does not need to be accompanied, have elaborate instructions, or use suggestions.

CLASSROOM VISITATIONS

Sometimes ideas, objects, and activities are not enough. A person is needed to help the teacher get the desired results. This person may have knowledge that the teacher does not possess, may be able to provide materials not available to the teacher, or may give a presentation that requires special talent. In this case it is necessary for the museum to send someone to the school, if the school cannot come to the museum.

All of these outreach programs require staff and an adequate budget. They have the advantage of reaching a large number of people that would not be reached otherwise. The programs using strictly materials require only an initial investment of time and money. The variety of educational programming is only limited by your imagination. One idea will lead to another. Something that you find in another museum can be adapted to your use. An article that you read can set off a whole new set of services for your organization. Examine each situation with an eye as to how you can modify, enlarge on, or improve to make it work for you. The result will be the development of a series of personalized educational programs for your institution.

Chapter 4
WORKING WITH PEOPLE

And in the time of their visitation they shall shine,
and run to and fro like sparks among the stubble.
Wisdom of Solomon — 7

NOTHING is so challenging, frustrating, or taken so much for granted as the fact that you must involve yourself with people to get your message across. Explaining how to work with people is like asking *What is life?* It can be all things to all people. To reach people you must make the information that you want them to retain pertinent. All of us, as human beings, have characteristics that we share. There are physical needs that must be met: the need for shelter, food, warmth. Basic emotions such as happiness, sadness, love, hate, anger are experienced by all. The use of the senses, sight, sound, smell, taste, and feelings, are basics that can be shared. By appealing to these shared needs and experiences, people will become involved. Sometimes a discussion calling on past experiences will be the best way to approach a group. At other times an appeal to a basic emotion is the most effective method. The part of the *Devil's advocate* is a role often used to make people justify and clarify their reasoning and feelings. Encouraging people to ask questions, verbalize their feelings, and share experiences are all ways to involve an individual. And this is what we want to do. Whether it is an individual, a tour group, a volunteer, a staff member, or another community organization, we want involvement and commitment. In this chapter, we will present some ideas to think about, useful approaches, and guidelines to evaluate your success in working with people.

When people (staff, volunteers, or visitors) come to your institution, what do they expect? What kind of public image do you have? Many people do not know what to expect from a museum. As far as learning is concerned, we come from a primarily print-oriented society with the library tradition instilled in us as we progress through the schools. Teacher education classes deal with how to use a library, students are taught from textbooks, and encouraged to do research using library facilities. Most schools and towns have libraries; therefore, printed materials become home ground. You feel comfortable using them, but this is not generally true of museums and objects; they continue to be special. Therefore, your institution's public image must become a welcoming one. It must become a place that is available to all segments of the community, that offers a variety of programs, and that does what it says it will do. This is not an easy task!

Learning is based upon learning, and one experience leads to another. One step at a time will work in the long run as well as a general overall reorganization. Something as simple as a place to sit in a gallery may show consideration for your visitors. A program at the local senior citizens center with a follow-up activity can welcome that group to your institution. Finally, your institution must be honest with staff, volunteers, and the public. Much has been written recently about professional ethics and the validity of collections. This is certainly important and must be honored; however, the honesty that we are concerned with is another facet of integrity. If you commit to a program, make sure that it is done. If your docent says he must leave by 11:30 a.m., make sure that he can. If there is a chance something may have to be cancelled, make sure that you set the conditions in the initial publicity.

Volunteers are one group of people that every museum has to work with in order to survive and to be effective. They come in all shapes, sizes, sex, religions, and educational and social backgrounds. They should be selected for their interests and abilities to fill certain positions. Whether your organization has a formalized volunteer organization or a one-to-one organizational structure, you still have to fit the volunteer to the needs. An interview with the potential volunteer is helpful in deciding how best to make use of their talents. Questions like the following, either written or discussed orally, will be useful in discovering what the volunteer is expecting. Make sure that they know there is no right or wrong answer. These are just general questions to help you both discover what the volunteer would like to get from the volunteer time invested.

General:

1. Why are you considering volunteering at this time?
2. What would the ideal volunteer job for you include?
3. What things would you *not* like to have included in your volunteer job? Why?
4. What do you expect to receive from this volunteer experience?
5. What personality traits or special abilities made you think that this institution would be a good place to be a volunteer?

Specific:

1. How do you feel about working in public contact areas? With adults? With children?
2. Do you like working with specifics: clerical work, filing, cataloging, research?
3. Do you work best with close supervision or do you prefer to be given a project and proceed on your own?
4. Are there personal conditions that will restrict your volunteer activities — health, family, schooling, job commitment?
5. Would you be willing to attend training sessions?

While these questions are being considered and answered, the interviewer should also be noting additional information such as the following:

1. What is the individual's reaction to the interview?
   — Volunteers information
   — Controlled — answers questions adequately
   — Evasive
   — Nervous
2. On first impression, the person seems to have
   — an outgoing, enthusiastic personality
   — controlled, no-nonsense approach
   — reserved, withdrawn

3. Speaker's voice is
   — easily understood, attractive
   — tends to ramble
   — low and hard to understand
4. What was the individual's reaction to taking additional training?
   — enthusiastic
   — willing, but cautious
   — felt it would not be necessary
5. Do you feel that this individual will complete commitment?
   — yes
   — no
   — maybe

As you will have realized by now, these questions could just as easily be used when employing paid staff, and this is just as it should be. To the public coming to your museum, it is not going to make any difference whether their contact person is paid or volunteer, they will make their judgment just the same. A museum offers marvelous volunteer opportunities; both behind the scenes and in front of the public. There are places for *the bubbles* and *the pillars* — those who enjoy people contact and those who find their satisfaction with research and statistics; those that are handy with tools and those who prefer working outdoors; or any combination of the above. With a little thought beforehand by the volunteer and the administration, a volunteer should be able to find a fulfilling volunteer experience. This does not mean that once a volunteer is placed in a job that he is there forever. Everyone responds to change, and a volunteer should be able to move up or try different areas. However, there is nothing quite as awkward as trying to redirect a volunteer who likes what he is doing and the administration doesn't. Preplanning through the interview process can help avoid this problem.

Both paid staff and volunteers need to know what is expected of them. Job descriptions will help in this respect. Of course, a general catchall phrase is always in museum work, such as *as needs require* or *as director requests* because running a museum is never cut and dried. But general guidelines are helpful.

Communication in any business or organization is essential. In large organizations, regularly scheduled departmental meetings with several general meetings throughout the year are necessary. In smaller organizations, lunch often becomes the time to find out what other staff members are doing. However, there should still be formally scheduled staff meetings. An in-house newsletter or memo system can also help to keep information available. Since there is so much interaction between departments or responsibilities, it is absolutely essential that people have a chance to ask questions, state their opinions, and voice complaints. A general overall knowledge of your institution is necessary for the maximum effectiveness of your programs to reach the public. The new exhibit area will not be effective if the researchers and interpreters do not communicate with the exhibit designers. (In some cases this is all the same person — but you have to be sure to look at it from all three angles.) There should also be a chain of command so that when a volunteer, visitor, or staff member has an idea or a complaint, there is a way to get action. An openness and availability to suggestions and ideas is important for a variety of reasons. Good ideas and suggestions often come from unexpected sources, and there should be a way to take advantage of these. Just as important is the fact that if there is no way to criticize or challenge, people can become frustrated or complacent. It is better to have the means before the occasion demands it. By that time, all too often, the personal feelings and emotions of individuals are involved. Take advantage of different personalities. Allow people to do assignments their own way since some people cannot talk to a group if they are tied to a script while others prefer to work within a very tight framework. Some people perform best under pressure or using an almost spur-of-the-moment approach; others need time to prepare. Take advantage of these characteristics, allow for flexibility, judge by the end results, and don't force a methodology mold onto the people you are working with.

All of the things that we have been thinking about can be used in the context of working with an individual person or with groups of people. But people in groups can react in ways that an individual person would never do. We have all worked with groups where everything clicked. People responded to you, each other and the situation just the way you wanted. It is a fantastic experience, but most of us have also worked with groups where nothing happened. There was no reaction, it was a ho-hum experience and everyone was relieved when it was over. What makes the difference? This is a hard question to answer. First of all we need to know ahead of time what we want to achieve with the group and how we hope to influence them to our goal or goals. Questions you might ask yourself while planning for the tour might be the following:

1. What would I like to see happen after working with this group? (a decision, a behavior change, a learning outcome)
2. What obstacles must I overcome to get this result? (negative feelings, incorrect information, apathy)
3. Why am I the person talking to this group? (superior knowledge, authority, reward, availability)
4. What are the best methods for influencing this group?
5. What positive signs can I expect if I am being successful?
6. What negative signs can I expect if I am not successful?
7. What can be done ahead of time to minimize these effects?

Eventually, you may not consciously ask yourself these questions, but they will be an instinctive reaction. After working with a group, you can go back over the questions and see where things went right or wrong. *Moving the group to a new area worked well when questions slowed up. I should have had an activity to show the concept I was trying to get across. I let the lady with the cane monopolize the discussion. I should have let the boy who knew so much about dinosaurs share his knowledge. I should have stopped talking fifteen minutes sooner. I should have. . .*

This type of informal evaluation of your own work with groups will help you learn your own strengths and weaknesses. Individuals also have a nonverbal language that they use. For example, if you notice people in your group yawning, playing with their hair, adjusting their clothing, or frowning, you can be sure you are losing your audience. These *defense* activities let you know that the person is withdrawing mentally, although still trapped physically by your tour. The same applies to people watching other activities in the area, staring into space, talking to others in the party, or lowering the head and refusing eye contact. Holding eye contact with a person encourages interaction between individuals; looking away discourages it.

The formation of your tour group can also influence participation. If your group is divided into small, nonformalized groups, they will tend to interact with just the smaller group. If you are talking with just a part of the group, those in the larger group may hesitate to become involved in the discussion because they feel they are intruding. The smaller fragmented groups may tend to drift away to pursue their own interests and conversations. However, this type of grouping may encourage others passing through an area to join a tour or an activity.

When a tour is more formalized, for example, standing in a circle or all seated together, the members of the group tend to feel a greater responsibility to the group activities. People coming into an area hesitate to join the more formalized group and will probably pass on through. Both types of group formations can be used effectively depending upon the objectives of the activity or tour you are conducting. Soon you will be able to anticipate how a group is going to react: who needs to be encouraged, who needs to be controlled, and what method is best to use to allow the objectives to be met. The ability to analyze the capabilities, skills, and interests of groups can come through experience. But there are some guidelines that are useful.

PIAGETIAN LEARNING LEVELS

Jean Piaget, a Swiss psychologist, has made a considerable impact upon the philosophy and rationale with respect to levels of learning and the chronological age of the learner. Piaget's fundamental thesis about knowledge is: *To know an object is to act on it.*[1] In other words, learning comes from the world and from the objects in it.

Children are producing and changing structures from birth through adulthood. Piaget has stated that *learning is possible only when there is active assimilation.*[2] Thus, assimilation leads

---

[1] Jean Piaget, "Development and Learning," *Journal of Research in Science Teaching,* 2, Issue 3 (New York, Wiley, 1964), pp. 176-186.
[2] Piaget, "Development and Learning," op. cit., p. 185.

to changes in structure. This change of structure occurs by analyzing, synthesizing, classifying, evaluating, comparing, and utilizing all of one's rational powers. Utilizing the learning model of Piaget enables docents to lead visitors (especially children) to achieve maximum cognitive learning potential.

The Piagetian learning model promotes the interaction of the learner with his environment via inquiry. Inquiry involves the seeking, receiving, and processing of information. In order to do this, the learner (museum visitor) must utilize all of the rational powers mentioned previously — classifying, etc.

There are several factors that affect the cognitive structure of the learner. Among these are the maturation process, social interaction, and experiences that the learner has had. According to Piaget, there are two aspects to experience: physical and logico-mathematical.[3] Physical experience relates to the learner interacting with objects in the learner's environment. This type of experience is essential for the very young learner (museum visitor). Physical experience is also needed by many adolescents because their intellectual development has not reached the point where experience involving logic has any meaning for them. Any adult who encounters something new will also attempt to first secure physical or interactive experiences in order to acquire the necessary information.

The second type of experience, logico-mathematical, allows the learner to recognize that when he counts five groups of two objects he arrives at the same total as when he counts two groups of five objects.

Piaget has also stated that *a child learns very little when experiments are performed for him. He must do them himself rather than sit and watch them done.*[4] Learning from logico-mathematical experiences takes place only when the actions are internalized, that is the learner takes the actions into his cognitive structure and is now able to make decisions based upon these internalized actions and not upon physical manipulations. The learner must also be able to internalize his actions and reverse his

---

[3]Jean Piaget, "Forward," Millie Almy, *Young Children's Thinking* (New York Teachers College Press, Columbia University, 1966), pp. v and vi.
[4]Ibid., p. vi

reasoning to proceed from one point in the line of reasoning back to the beginning. It is important to note that children in their early years of school cannot reverse their thinking, which explains why they should not have logico-mathematical experiences.

You may now ask, *What does all of this have to do with being a docent or working with visitors?* The implications of Piaget's work upon museum education are immense. In museum education programs, emphasis must be placed upon the learner (visitor) interacting. This means that the docent must ascertain the visitor's level of language development and then provide experiences in accordance with this language and maturity level so that the visitor will be able to retain and sharpen his learning about a particular object, event, or occurrence. The docent must provide the museum visitor with a maximum of activity to investigate and interact with the material being presented. Piaget summarized his concern by stating, *In the area of logico-mathematical structures, children have real understanding only of that which they invent themselves, and each time that we try to teach them something too quickly, we keep them from reinventing it themselves.* [5]

Piaget is most famous for popularizing the notion of stages of intellectual development. That is, it is possible to document and identify the stages and ages for the development of thought. There are four major periods in Piaget's account of the development of thought. They are the sensory-motor phase, which extends from birth to about two and one-half years of age; the preoperational level, which goes from about two and one-half to seven years of age; the concrete operational period, which extends from about seven to twelve years of age; and the formal operational level, which begins at about eleven or twelve years of age. It is possible to formally evaluate the performance of children and adults to determine the actual Piagetian level of development. However, keep in mind that the divisions between any one level of cognitive development are not absolute boundaries and that even though individual children and adults may be the same age chronologically, they may also be at different levels of cognitive development.

---

[5] Ibid., p. vi.

It is helpful for museum educators to be able to recognize some of the general characteristics of the various learning levels in order to design better activities and tours for visitors. Table 4-I indicates the general Piagetian Intellectual Development Levels including the developmental stage, general age range, and a sampling of characteristics related to that stage.

As you review Table 4-I it is important to note that unless a learner has ample and proper concrete operational experiences at that level, he *will not* become formal operational. That is, he will not be able to make decisions that require abstract thinking. The research evidence collected to date strongly suggests that most of our educational institutions including museums are not providing the experiences needed at the concrete operational level that will enable learners to become formal operational. It has also been found that many educators and docents are providing formal operational experiences for concrete operational learners and the result is that little, if any, learning is taking place.

To summarize, the docent needs to provide the museum visitor with opportunities for cognitive growth in three realms of experience. First, is social experience; that is the experience of confronting views and ideas of other children and adults. This serves as an important force in overcoming egocentrism by stimulating the child to consider and adapt to other points of view.

Second, there is physical experience. This consists of activities that involve exploring the properties, such as color, weight, form, and movement in space of the objects.

Third, logico-mathematical experiences are extremely important for the development of the transition from concrete to formal operational. Children have real understanding only of that which they are encouraged to invent themselves.

The most valuable aspect of Piaget's work is not his delineation of the various stages of intellectual development, but rather his portrayal of how children go about learning. There is a danger in focusing only upon the stages for it too readily leads to attempts to categorize children rather than to observe them in action. Each stage should be viewed as legitimate in its own right, for the ways of learning of each stage make necessary contributions to capabilities at later ages. We hope that this overview of

TABLE 4-1

PIAGETIAN INTELLECTUAL DEVELOPMENT LEVELS

Stage of Development: Sensory-motor

General Age Range: Birth to 30 months

GENERAL CHARACTERISTICS

—Motor skills unevenly developed.	—Asks countless questions.	—Needs to learn to give and take.
—Rapid language development.	—Learning what is acceptable behavior and what is not.	—Needs simple, clear routines and limited choices.
—Constantly active.	—Needs time, patience, interest and guidance from adults.	—Hidden objects located via random, physical searching.
—Shows fatigue.		
—Great curiosity.		

TABLE 4-I (continued)

Stage of Development: Preoperational

General Age Range: 30 months to 7 years

GENERAL CHARACTERISTICS

—Good general motor control being developed.	—Interested in group activity.	—Has difficulty making decisions.
—High activity level.	—Needs opportunities for plenty of activity.	—Boys' and girls' interests begin to differ.
—Increasing attention span.	—Needs opportunities to do things him/herself.	—Needs wise supervision with a minimum of interference.
—Handedness established.	—Needs to learn about world by seeing and doing things.	—Help in developing acceptable manners and habits.
—Home centered.	—Eager to learn.	—Needs encouragement.
—Eager and able to carry out some responsibility.	—Learns best through active participation.	—Lacks operational reversibility in thought and action
—Purposeful and constructive.	—Inept at activities using small muscles.	
—Uses language well—enjoys dramatic play.		

TABLE 4-I (continued)

Stage of Development: Concrete Operational

General Age Range: 7 years to 12 years

GENERAL CHARACTERISTICS		
—Eyes ready for near and far vision.	—Perfectionist—wants to do well, but loses interest if discouraged or pressured.	—Reasonable explanations without talking down.
—Large muscles still developing.		—Active rough and tumble play.
—Attention span getting longer.	—Wide discrepancies in reading ability.	—Concepts of reversibility develops.
—Eye-hand coordination good—ready for crafts and shop work by 9 or 10.	—Thinking is concrete rather than abstract.	—Unable to isolate variables and proceeds from step to step in thinking without relating steps to each other
—Often careless, noisy, argumentative, but also alert, friendly, interested in people.	—Fond of team games, comics, television, movies, adventure stories, collections.	
—Individual differences become distinct, abilities now apparent.	—Needs praise and encouragement from adults.	

TABLE 4-I (continued)

Stage of Development: Formal Operational

General Age Range: 11 to 12 years and Beyond

GENERAL CHARACTERISTICS		
—Hypothetical-deductive reasoning develops. —Development of the ability to perform controlled experiments. —Girls usually two years ahead of boys in physical development. —Wide range of individual differences in maturity level.	—Marked interest differences between boys and girls. —Opinion of one's own group valued more than that of adults. —Self-conscious about physical changes. —Needs opportunities for greater independence.	—Needs warm affection and sense of humor in adults. —No nagging, condemnation or talking down. —Needs opportunities to make decisions. —Can think in the abstract.

Piagetian learning levels will assist you in designing a museum education program that will respond to your visitors so that worthwhile and productive learning can take place.

While this information is useful in planning learning programs, we must still remember to consider the differences in our visiting groups as well as the similarities. Young children usually come to the museum in controlled groups, such as with a class, a scout group, or their family. Learning activities for a child are centered about adding to the knowledge they already have for use at some future date, for some future need. Adult groups are usually seeking to meet a more immediate need. There is also a general pattern that adults seem to follow. Young adults tend to be motivated by career-oriented programs, items that deal with a family situation or role, and crisis situations. The crisis can be of a personal, community, national, or international nature. Often they are seeking particular knowledge that can be applied to one of the above situations. As a person reaches middle age there seems to be a change in focus. They gradually come to realize that the future they have been orienting their lives toward is the *here and now.* They have reached the stage where certain expectations should have happened if they are going to. It really makes no difference whether they have been successful or not — it still becomes a period of reassessment. The focus then becomes more of a *Who-am-I?, Where-am-I?* attitude. Interests tend toward hobbies, the immediate world around them, special talents or interests, attention to values, and humanistic concerns. The senior citizen group shares the above concerns but has an added dimension. They have a sense of personal experience of having seen trends develop and social problems reoccur; they have a sense of continuity that can be used and developed.

As we look at these characteristics, we notice that the lives of most people seem to be periods of stability punctuated by role changing events. Major changes or events seem to activate the periods of adaptation, growing, and learning. It would appear that a museum's multifaceted programs should have a great impact on adult audiences since museums do have many advantages in reaching this audience. They are a place where you can get the *feel* of the community, meet people with similar interests, and cut across socioeconomic boundaries. The lack of structure and the openness of programming allows for interest groups to organize. There is no better atmosphere to cultivate learning for the joy of learning. However, there may also be some barriers to remove before this audience can be reached at its full potential. Adults must choose to participate since the incentive of school credit or career advancement is usually not applicable. Facilities may not be easily accessible and parking may be difficult, and since physical barriers may keep some out, safety factors must be considered. There is also the problem of self-concept, peer pressure, and the fact that needs of the planner may not meet the needs of the participant. Adults are the most challenging and necessary group for any institution to attract. They are your supporters, board members, volunteers, and main body of visitors. The challenges and the rewards are equally important.

Generalizations are helpful in planning, but remember to keep them in the proper perspective — as a useful tool and a guideline, not as an absolute. Once you have people in your institutions, what exactly do you do with them? What is the nitty-gritty of conducting a tour?

GUIDELINES FOR CONDUCTING A SMOOTH TOUR

Report for the tour at least ten minutes early:
— This will give you a chance to prepare yourself for the tour group and not appear hurried or flustered. Of course it is assumed that you are already prepared informationally for the tour and have checked the area to make sure there are no changes since your last tour.

Start your tour with a positive attitude:
— No matter what your personal feelings may be, remember that your first responsibility is to the tour. A fight with your spouse, a car that needs repair, a visit to the dentist — all of these problems must be pushed aside when you are giving a tour. You are the visitors contact with the institution. Your attitude will be largely responsible for the kind of experience the visitor will have.

Always introduce yourself to the tour:
— This is just common courtesy; it makes you seem more *real*. If you are role playing, you of course use that name.

Otherwise, use whatever you would like to have them call you — Mrs. Woods, Jeanette, Jerry; anything's better than *Hey you!*

Inform the tour of any specific rules or safety precautions:

— Let the tour know what is expected of them. Examples: no smoking rules, physical safety factors — a river on the site or a steep bank to be avoided; inform them of participation activities that require special notice — open fire, hot metal, hot wax.

Keep your attention focused on your tour group:

— Do not start visiting with just one person on the tour or with other staff members; be available for questions.

When standing to talk with a group, remember —

— You are going to have to move the group — don't get trapped in the middle or the back.

— Be in a position that enables you to keep the entire group under surveillance for safety and security reasons.

— Watch sun if outside or lights inside — do not force a group to look into a light source.

When moving a tour —

— Keep your tour together and watch for stragglers — this is important for control, safety of the group, and security reasons.

— Always lead your group and let them know when, where, and how you are going to move. Be explicit.

— Be alert and flexible while moving your group. Change routes as the occasion demands — a hall being mopped or a hole being dug.

— If you want a group to sit or kneel — tell them so and then wait until they are settled before continuing.

— If giving a group *free time* to explore let them know where you will be, when they should rejoin the tour, and where you will be at that time.

When closing a tour —

— Try not to leave anyone in the group with any *important* questions.

— If you enjoyed the group — tell them so.

— Invite them back to the site — give them the hours you are open or an upcoming event that might be interesting to them.

— Inform them of how to exit the site and remain with the group until they are out of your area of responsibility.

GUIDELINES TO HELP TOUR INTERPRETATION

Develop a pleasant rapport with the group:

— A smile or question about the trip will help to set the tone.

Tailor your tour to the group; avoid giving *canned tours* at the same pace or in the same voice:

— Talk to the group leader and learn about any special interests or background work that the group may have.

— Focus your attention on the group — not the leader. Speak to individuals — ask them nonfactual, opinion questions that enable you to discover *where the group is at* and where you may want to go. Let them know you are interested in knowing what they think by asking questions and learning their opinions.

Keep your interpretation flexible and individual, but accurate.

— No tour should ever be expected to listen to all you know on a subject. Choose information that seems to be applicable to the particular group.

— Although all docents will have received approximately the same information and training, present it in the way that is most comfortable for you and best meets the needs of your tour.

— Beware of *visitor input* and *good stories*. Never insert information into your tour without checking for accuracy.

— If there are qualifiers about information, be sure to include them in your tour. *This ought to be. . . Current research shows. . .*

— If you are asked a question you cannot answer, do not be afraid to say you do not know. Never guess or try to bluff your way through. You may suggest another source of information like the library. Or if you think it worthwhile, you could research it and send the group a follow-up letter.

A group will show more interest in an exhibit or an object if the docent allows them to make discoveries. Guide them by asking questions and try not to give too many answers.

— Increase the sense of reality about an object or exhibit by asking —

What is this?

Who would have been here or used this?

What would they have been doing?

How would they have used this object?

Why is it made out of this material?

— Dates for their own sake are generally not too important; make a time period meaningful by association:

What was life like during this period?

How did people travel, get food, and dress?

What conditions caused this event?

Who was involved?

What other things happened because of this event?

— If a specific personality is involved ask —

What type of personality was he?

How did he live?

What was his background?

What did he like? Not like?

What influence did he have?

Be sensitive to the *feel* of the group.

— Divide into smaller groups if that seems the best way to get the desired response.

— Assign each small group a problem to solve and have them report back to the larger group.

— Concentrate on areas that seem to have their interest; then tie them into larger concepts.

— Move the group as their interest indicates; you don't want them to feel either rushed or bored. Pay attention to their reaction, but keep in mind your own overall time allotment.

— Use methods such as games, searches, movement, and whatever seems desirable by group reaction.

— If using handling materials, ask one person to describe it in detail and then involve the rest of the group by asking if they agree. Appeal to the use of all the senses. Accept almost any reasonable answer.

HOW DO YOU MEASURE THE SUCCESS OF YOUR TOUR?

If the group has enjoyed interacting with their surroundings and you, you can feel that your tour was a success. If they have shown interest, enthusiasm, and excitement during the tour and have left still wanting more, you know you have given a good tour.

Questions that you could ask yourself about the tour might include the following:

— Was the vocabulary and the content appropriate?
— Has the information retained its accuracy?
— Was the presentation fresh and enthusiastic?
— Did the tour format allow enough flexibility to meet the needs of the group?
— What was the audience response? (attentive, restless, dialogue)
— Was the group under control?
— What was my attitude toward the tour? Did it come across that way?

Questions that you could ask about yourself as a docent are listed below:

— Could a tape recorder replace me?
— Did I adjust and respond to the tour group?
— Did I see the tour from the visitor's point of view?
— Do I continue to increase my knowledge, explore, and learn?
— Do I communicate with other docents and staff?
— Am I receptive to suggestions and changes?
— Am I aware of the total program of this institution and its needs?

Now that we have discussed how to give a tour and how to evaluate your own tour and performance; there are some other aspects of your tour program that also must be mentioned. The mechanics of organizing your program are important. People must know what programs are available, how to schedule, and what is expected of their group before and after the initial contact. You must know your own procedures and through record keeping, exactly how the program is progressing.

COMMUNICATION

Community groups need to know what you have to offer them. This can be accomplished through letters, personal contact, media announcements, or general mailings. Any or all of these methods may be effective, but you have to get the word out. Remember that all organizations have their own chain of command and rules. Honor these at all times and work within their framework. Almost any school system wants you to start at the top, but do not stop there. The superintendent should be contacted, but the classroom teacher is the person you have to reach. This may mean that you have to go from the central administrator to the curriculum person to the building principal and then the department head before you can reach the classroom teacher, but that teacher is the necessary contact.

Local media is often happy to help you inform the public about your programs, but you cannot expect the radio station to give you free public service announcements when you buy an ad in the local newspaper. Other community organizations may want to take advantage of your services, but they do not want you to *take over* their program. All organizations, even your own, have their own procedures and protocol that have been developed because of past experiences. Even though following protocol is sometimes frustrating and time consuming, it is the best way to get cooperation.

HOW TO SCHEDULE A TOUR

Each institution must decide the best method for scheduling their tours. Factors that must be taken into consideration are the number of tours being scheduled, the number of sites being booked, other activities being offered by the institution, staff available for the processing method, and amount of information needed by the institution. But any method chosen must be consistent and able to be communicated to both those desiring the tours and the staff that does the actual booking. Some institutions prefer to do all booking by verbal communications. This way any questions can be answered at the time the tour is booked. Date and time can be confirmed and you can be sure that all pertinent data is obtained. Other institutions prefer to use only written communications. This means that there may need to be several communications before a date and time can be agreed upon, but it also means that there will not be a lot of staff time tied up with phone conversations.

Both methods have drawbacks:
— Verbal communications are not always understood the same way by both parties.
— Verbal communication means that there is nothing to refer to at a later date if a question arises.
— Record keeping can be more difficult if information is not recorded in a consistent manner.
— Written communication does not lend itself as well to answering questions by teachers at the desired time.
— Written communication may require several exchanges before the tour can be confirmed.

Therefore, it would seem that the best scheduling method would be a combination of both the verbal and written methods. This allows a person to call or write to check dates, time, type of tours, and any questions; then the person can fill in a written request form that can be filed by the institution for future referal and record keeping. The institution then sends a written confirmation to act as a check that the information is correct and as a reminder of the tour.

The tour request form (Figure 4-1) should be designed so that it is easy to understand and to quickly fill out. It allows for several tours to be scheduled at one time, provides necessary information, and allows flexibility in scheduling.

TOUR RECORDS

It is important to keep complete records of the tour program. A variety of information about your tour will be important for your institution's planning. Basic information that should be recorded:
— How many tours are given?
— What types of tours are requested?
— Is your tour audience coming from a specific area?

Return to:
                                        A single tour or
    Museum Address   a combination of any
    Telephone Number   two one-hour tours
                                        may be scheduled
                                        any week day.

School or Organization _____

Mailing Address _____ Zip _____

Person in Charge _____ Telephone (area code)___ - ___ -

Grade or Level _____ Number of Children _____

Number of Adults _____ Number of Buses _____

                Gift Shop Open ( ) yes   ( ) no

    Tour Requested   Time   Try-it Activity

1. _____

2. _____

3. _____

Date

    1st Choice   2nd Choice   3rd Choice

1. _____

2. _____

3. _____

        There is a 50¢ fee per person for all tours. Please
bring it in a labeled envelope and give it to your docent.

        Fee _____ x .50 = _____

            Number attending   Total

    Additional forms may be obtained from the Museum; or
this form may be copied.

Figure 4-1. Tour Request Form

— Are the number of people on tours growing or declining?
— Is the general overall tour program growing or declining?
— What docents are giving tours? How many?

    Additional information that you might want to record could
include the following:

— New tours added and their effect upon the overall program

— Outside influences on program — other institutions, school finances, cost of living
— Changes in tour procedures — charging for tours, admission increases, hours open
— What period of the year is most popular for tours? Why?
— What time of the day is most popular?

After you have determined the information you want to record, a standardized form should be designed. This form should be kept as simple as possible to allow you to pull information as desired. By standardizing the method of recording all tours, you can compare one type of tour to another, one year to another and all tours offered by your organization even if they include more than one site.

USE OF TOUR RECORDS BY THE INSTITUTION

Tour Selection

Knowing what tours are receiving the most participation can help you in planning new tours or in culling out those that are not meeting the needs of your audience. No program should remain static. If the records show that your general tour is no longer being requested, even though it was the most popular one two years ago, it should be obvious that something has changed.

Possible considerations could be the following:

— The school curriculum has changed and the specialized tour now meets their needs.
— The tour was so well received in the past that all of your potential audience has been on the tour, and you have not made any changes in the tour format to create a new audience.
— Outside influences are affecting your program:
  — The school budget no longer allows for field trips.
  — Another museum is offering a similar tour and doing a better job.
— Your *Come and Find* tour covers approximately the same information but allows for more student participation. Even though it is a longer tour, the teachers are choosing it because they feel it is a more worthwhile experience for their classes.

Additional research will be necessary to determine what is causing the change. Once the cause has been determined, then necessary adjustments can be made.

Ages of Tour Participants

You feel that you are doing an excellent job of meeting the needs of elementary school children and senior citizens. The number of tours for both age groups are growing. Yet, when you compile your tour report at the end of the year, you suddenly realize that the majority of your elementary tours are fourth through sixth grade. You have lost almost all of the kindergarten through third grade tours. The overall number of tours did not show that the composition of your tour participants had greatly changed. Again, you will want to look for reasons.

Areas of Participation

Keeping records of where you are getting your tour participants may reveal new audiences, help you decide how to slant tour information, and show weaknesses in your communication methods. For example you may find that you are doing an excellent job of reaching the rural schools in your area, but that the city schools are not using your services. Private schools might not appear for tours because the tour materials are not being sent to them since they are not on the general mailing list. A school system that had used the services frequently in the past might have had a personnel change, and you will need to make a new contact visit.

Record keeping could show that schools outside a fifty mile radius are now feeling the effect of transportation costs and are no longer able to travel to your site. Or conversely, schools in your area are now coming to your site since they are no longer able to make a trip to the state capitol museum.

Time of Tours

A record of the time, days of the week, and months that tours occur will help you plan your tour year. An outdoor site may discover that they are being used primarily as a culminating activity at the end of the school year. May and June are so heavily scheduled that tours have to be turned away, but September and October are a slow time for the site. Therefore, by planning programs that are to be used as initiating activities, they can spread tour activities and serve the audience equally as well. If Tuesday and Friday prove to be the most popular tour days, then staff can be assigned accordingly. Travel time to and from a site may have an effect upon who can schedule a tour or even if you want to have an early time slot. Investigation may show that the reason January is such a slow tour month is because the school curriculum does not allow the teacher enough time for field trips. Therefore, this might be an excellent time for in-service training at the museum. Your institution has assumed that July is a slow tour month because schools in your area are not in session. However, records show that other community groups are now using your services to such an extent that July is now one of your busiest tour periods.

Patterns of Attendance

A simple count of the number of tours you are conducting will not reveal any of the changes that we have been discussing. However, a count of the number of tours and attendance can be useful. It may be used to show if your program is growing or declining. Please note that both number of tours and attendance is specified. You may find that the number of your tours remain static, but your attendance figure will go up. Schools may be finding it necessary to *fill the bus* before they will allow a class to take a field trip. Or you may find that as the school population declines your number of tours will again remain static, but your attendance will be smaller.

It is necessary to keep records over a number of years to get a true picture for comparison. One year you may show an increase of fifty tours and you feel that your program is growing; the next year you note that you are down fifty tours and you wonder what happened; then the following year those same fifty tours reappear. It has taken three years to realize that fifty teachers in your area are rotating your museum with another museum for field trips.

Other occurrences that can influence record keeping might be a bad winter that curtails two months of tours, the opening of a new gallery that pulls in a large number of first visits, or a remodeling project at your institution that makes it inconvenient for groups to visit.

Staff and Budget Requirements

Obviously, record keeping can be used to indicate staff and budgetary needs. Records can help to justify new staff or cutbacks, to show you where seasonal help might be needed, to indicate if supplies should be increased or cut back, and to give you facts to present to the administration and/or the board. Tour records will also help you explain why it might be necessary to charge a fee for tours or to increase an admission price, what new programs need to be started and why, how activities should be expanded or curtailed, and what results could be expected. Having the records to refer to gives you actual information rather than a feeling that something is or is not happening. However, to make record keeping reliable it must be standardized, accurate, and maintained.

DOCENT USE OF TOUR RECORDS

Careful analyzation of guided visit scheduling information by the docent can provide insight into the group. Typical scheduling information might include the following:
— The name of the school or group
— The school or group's address
— The name of the city
— The grade level or group interest
— The selected guided visit
— The number in the group
— Date of the scheduled visit
— Time of the scheduled visit
— Additional information about the group

The name of the school or group reveals whether it is private, public, or church affiliated and can often suggest the group's level of achievement and religious views and beliefs. The school or group's address and the city where it's located can tell whether it is an urban, suburban, rural, or out-of-state school or group. Given this information, the docent can discern the group's familiarity with the museum and generalize about the group's expectations and traits. For instance, rural groups generally have visited the museum infrequently in contrast to urban groups who are more frequent museum visitors. The docent can also speculate about the group's skills, interest, and traits after learning of the location. The size of the group can help the docent select and structure activities for the group. The smaller the size of the group the more numerous and varied the activity options. The additional information can tell the docent if special teaching techniques must be used. This scheduling information will state if the group is gifted, disabled, or has learning disabilities. It will also indicate if there is an exhibit or exhibits that the group is especially interested in visiting and if they have a special area of interest. The name of the selected guided visit aids the docent in establishing a focus and selecting concepts to be discussed during the visit.

The date of the visit informs the docent of the season the visit will occur and if it will take place before a holiday, vacation, or on a Friday. Groups visiting the museum before a holiday, on a Friday, or in the spring are sometimes much more restless and have shorter attention spans than groups visiting on other days and times of the year. Visits scheduled in the spring may be part of an itinerary that includes visits to other places of interest as well, and the visitors may be tired and restless by the time they reach the museum. Whether a visit is scheduled in the morning or afternoon suggests to the docent how a group might react. Groups scheduled in the morning may be more alert and eager while afternoon groups may be fatigued and not nearly as enthusiastic.

A careful examination of the schedule can help the docent anticipate the group's interests, abilities, attitudes, and actions. The scheduling information can also suggest how to structure the visit and influence the selection of the interpretative techniques to be used during the visit. It is important that the docent view the plan that evolves from the scheduling information as tentative. Only when the docent is actually interacting with the group in the museum environment can he engage in responsive interpretation.

WORKING WITH OTHER COMMUNITY GROUPS

Often we become so involved with our own programs that we forget how we can help other community groups and how other groups in the community can help us. Too often there seems to be a feeling of competition between the history museum and the art museum, the *Y* camp and the children's classes, and the symphony and the summer arts festival. And it must be admitted that there is competition for volunteers, participants or audiences, and monies. But there is the more important aspect of shared talents, shared impact, and shared effort that offers more effective programming opportunities. Often a shared event is easier to stage and has a greater impact upon the community than a series of competing events. A large festival needs the supporting efforts of smaller organizations to make their event possible; the smaller organizations need the monies that they can earn during the festival to carry on their activities during the rest of the year. All can benefit.

A joint series of programs sponsored by the art museum, the symphony, and the history museum could explore all facets of a subject — giving it more dimension than looking at it strictly from the viewpoint of a musician, artist, or historian. An arts festival featuring sculpture, painting, music, drama, and choral renditions may attract a much greater audience than a concert. This is not to say that each community group should not maintain its own special interest and personality but only that joint projects can be complimentary and beneficial to all.

Smaller projects also offer possibilities:
- A garden club could plant a flower bed on the museum's grounds.
- The historical museum could offer a *badge day* for the local scout organization.
- Members at the Senior Citizens Center could be interviewed for the library's oral history collection.

— A preservation group could help local businesses research their buildings.
— Gift shops could sell products made at the sheltered workshop.

Larger organizations with their own facilities can help smaller groups in the community by offering them a place to perform, and at the same time they will be supplementing their own programs. A *Music at the Museum* series can offer performers an opportunity to appear before the community without the necessity of renting a hall. It also brings a potential *new* audience into the museum. A *reader's theater group* can offer a new experience for a children's activity.

While opportunities for sharing are endless and the benefits are many, it must also be admitted that there are problems involved in working with other organizations. It is often difficult to settle on a date, to agree on objectives, and to coordinate efforts. The first objective of any joint project should be a clear understanding by all parties of responsibilities, deadlines, and duties. Then there must be a commitment by all members to meet these obligations.

Working with people is important:
— Every individual that comes to your institution
— Every person that takes a tour
— Every organization member that contacts you
— Every staff member that you work with
— Every person that volunteers time

These are the important people. These are the ones you must work with. Enthusiasm, knowledge, consideration, and interest are your tools. The very existence of your organization depends upon the ability to work with people.

Chapter 5
WORKING WITH SPECIAL GROUPS

Give me a fish and I eat for a day.
Teach me to fish and I eat for a lifetime.
— Traditional

IF a docent is to modify his interpretive presentation so that
it responds to the needs of the museum's special audiences,
he must possess a clear understanding of the characteristics that
set these special visitors apart from the typical museum visitor. It
is not enough for the docent to become merely aware of the differences among the various special audiences, but he must also
translate those differences into meaningful interpretive interactions within the museum. There are four elements influencing
the design of the interpretive interaction:
- Learner
- Docent
- Information or concepts to be learned
- Interpretive techniques
The following special museum visitors will be discussed: the
young child, the gifted and talented, the visually impaired, the
hearing impaired, the mentally handicapped, the physically disabled, adolescents, nonschool groups, and special interest groups.
It is hoped that a clearer insight into the traits, limitations, special needs, and capabilities of these special groups will enable the
docent to structure a meaningful guided visit for them.

THE YOUNG CHILD

Young children in grades kindergarten through second are distinctly different from their older counterparts, and successful interpretation requires that the docent have a clear understanding of those differences. Some common characteristics of young children are given below:

— Very active, not good at sitting
— Egocentric, everything is viewed from their personal perspective and needs
— Highly imaginative, difficulty distinguishing reality from fantasy
— Concrete, unable to master conceptual thinking and reasoning skills
— Nonreaders or those having only minimal reading skills
— Neophytes, new to most learning experiences

Learning for the young child should be an active process with emphasis upon *doing*. Knowledge and awareness are acquired largely through the child's sensory exploration of his environment. Seeing, hearing, touching, tasting, and smelling are important ways of learning for this age group. Previous personal experiences influence and help delineate the child's perceptions. As a result, the learning environment must be rich with numerous and varied stimuli providing concrete experiences, which form the basis for eventual abstract thinking.

In structuring activities for this age group the docent must focus upon learning through discovery. Effective learning activities are characterized by sensory involvement and exploration. The activities should capitalize upon the child's personal fantasies and experiences. Lecturing as a mode of teaching must be minimized and instead firsthand involvement encouraged. Playing, fantasizing, observing, comparing, classifying, reasoning, and judging are important learning tasks for the young child and should be incorporated into museum activities. The docent should include songs, finger plays, stories, picture books, and other related activities in the guided visit format since children respond readily to them.

It is important that the docent remember that the young child will often move very slowly and deliberately. Being the line leader, maintaining assigned line positions, and remaining with their partner throughout the guided visit are important for this age child. Even in the museum setting their teacher remains the final authoritarian figure for them and his wishes, rules, and organization must be respected by the docent to avoid creating a stressful situation for the children.

THE GIFTED AND TALENTED

The gifted and talented represent approximately 20 to 30 percent of the total population. Properly nurtured, their special intellectual and creative gifts may one day result in new inventions, discoveries, and alternative life-styles for society. However, unidentified raw potential remains underdeveloped and largely unproductive. If the gifted mind is to expand and grow, stimulation is essential, and society must provide every opportunity for the development of these unique thinkers and doers.

Early recognition of the talented is the first step toward structuring meaningful learning experiences. But identification of gifted potential is a complex process involving both subjective and objective measurements. Giftedness should be interpreted as broadly as possible including not only intellectual abilities, but also talents and creativity. Some common characteristics of the gifted appear below:

- Highly curious
- Keen memory — but while capable of remembering much information, strict rote or mere factual information is not in keeping with their mode of thinking
- Extensive vocabulary
- Intense concentration
- Empathy with others
- Heightened perceptions — resulting in increased awareness of both joy and pain, and the discrepancy between the ideal and reality
- Recognition of patterns and relationships
- Aptitude for divergent thinking
- Rapid comprehension

Giftedness can take many forms and is reflected in outstanding performance or potential ability in any of the following areas:
— General intellectual ability
— Specific academic aptitude
— Creative thinking — gauged by the number of creative ideas and amount of flexibility in the thinking presented
— Leadership
— Visual and performing arts
— Psychomotor ability

Many educational institutions virtually ignore or at best only superficially recognize nonacademic giftedness.

I.Q., Intelligence Quotient, tests are diagnostic tools which attribute a numerical score to intelligence. The tests are designed to measure how much a person can learn. They assign a score representing a person's mental age and compare it with the person's chronological age. That score is then compared with the scores of others of the same age. Intellectual ability is not equally distributed and is limited genetically and neurologically, with some minds being more capacious than others. The Stanford-Binet I. Q. tests establish the following categories for above average ability:
— The Academically Talented — above 115 I. Q. representative of approximately 16 percent of the population
— Superior Intelligence — above 125 I. Q. representative of approximately 5 percent of the population
— Gifted Intelligence — above 140 I. Q. representative of approximately 0.6 percent of the population
— Highly Gifted — above 160 I. Q. representative of approximately 0.007 percent of the population

For comparison purposes the average I. Q. falls between 90 and 110.

Intelligence is a combination of both heredity and environment, since a person's inherited ability is influenced by his environment. Due to their limitations, I. Q. tests should not be the only diagnostic tool used to reveal giftedness. The tests cannot separate innate intelligence from environmental differences. It is almost impossible for the tests to distinguish between what a person already knows and what he can learn. In addition I. Q. tests are incapable of detecting and evaluating creative ability. To determine giftedness, a variety of diagnostic methods must be used. The following are some of the methods used to identify the gifted and talented child:

— Standardized I. Q. tests
— Creativity tests
— Teacher nomination
— Sociometric tests
— Parent and peer nomination
— Self-nomination

Without adult intervention the gifted child is likely to concentrate exclusively upon his particular area of giftedness resulting in a lack of balance. But if other potential abilities are not to be overlooked, the gifted child's interests must remain broad and he must be introduced to varied experiences and ways of thinking and urged to participate in different activities. Because of their extraordinary ability, the gifted are sometimes viewed as self-educators. Boredom is an especially critical problem for the gifted, and many see extra work as a panacea, when in reality it often is a way of penalizing the child for his talents. These children need to grow not only intellectually but socially and emotionally as well.

Gifted children have an enormous capacity for receiving and retaining information, but they also need opportunities for applying the information. The talented must be trained and encouraged to be independent and original thinkers. Learning must be largely self-directed inquiry, incorporating problem-solving activities and experimentation. Generating ideas, elaborating upon them, working out the details, and testing them out are important learning experiences. The habit of evaluating information and analyzing cause and effect should also be cultivated. The forming of lifelong seekers of knowledge is the ultimate educational goal for the intellectually gifted.

The gifted and talented require programs different from those provided by the regular school program. There are three approaches that have been used in educating the gifted: acceleration, segregation, and enrichment. Acceleration has been the traditional choice and is characterized by early admission to first grade, bypassing a grade, participation in advanced placement programs, and taking college courses while still in high school. Accelerating a gifted child's program allows him to progress at a more rapid rate than his peers. But there can be social and emotional drawbacks to separating the child from his peer group and placing him with older but intellectually equal classmates. The decision to accelerate a child's program must consider his social adjustment as well as his academic progress. Segregation results in the creation of separate programs for the gifted. It involves removing the student from the regular school and placing him in a special school for the gifted and talented or establishing special classes within the regular school. Enrichment is broadening the basic course of study to provide a more varied and in-depth programming. Independent projects, extracurricular activities, and weekend projects are examples of enrichment programs. When developing programs for the gifted, these three approaches may be used separately or in combination with each other.

The museum can provide enrichment programs for the gifted and talented school population. It is programming that makes use of the museum staff's expertise and the museum environment. The goal is to provide a variety of learning experiences that increase the student's awareness and independent thinking. The docent should engage the students in such activities as defining, questioning, observing, classifying, generalizing, verifying, and applying. This results in the generation of information, which allows for a great variety of interpretation. The museum staff can then help the students develop a tolerance for ambiguity and to view a problem or situation in light of multiple causation.

THE HANDICAPPED

The handicapped population wish to maximize their independence and self-sufficiency so that they can participate more fully in community life. There are two legislative acts that mandate open access in public facilities for the handicapped. The 1968 Architectural Barriers Act, Public Law 90-480, requires that any public facility built or substantially renovated since 1968 and receiving federal support must be fully accessible to handicapped visitors and staff. On the other hand, the 1973 Rehabilitation

Act, Public Law 93-112, states that no federally supported activity can exclude the handicapped because their facilities are inaccessible. It becomes evident that if the museum is to serve the community it must include the handicapped among its audiences. Museums must be committed to providing exhibits, programs, and experiences that meet the unique needs of the handicapped visitor. No two handicapped persons are alike, and each has individual characteristics and needs, and many have multiple handicaps. The largest handicapped group who will visit the museum is that of the mentally handicapped, and the smallest groups are the visual and hearing impaired.

There are some common problems that a docent faces when interacting with the handicapped. They are how to react to the physical and/or mental differences and how to communicate and accept the handicapped as a person. It is essential that docents providing guided visits for the handicapped possess receptive attitudes. As nearly as possible handicapped visitors should receive the same museum experiences as any other visitors. Training of the museum docent should include sessions in which they learn about the characteristics and stereotypes of the handicapped, those teaching techniques that are most effective with the handicapped, and opportunities for confronting their personal fears, attitudes, and views of the handicapped person. The docent should —

— Be accepting of the handicapped as individuals
— Treat them as normally as possible
— Analyze their physical and mental capabilities
— Remain enthusiastic and relaxed throughout the visit

Generally the smaller the group, the more effective the guided visit, and groups as a rule should be no larger than ten. The docent should not abdicate to the other adults accompanying the group his role as an interpreter. When working with the handicapped population the docent must —

— Be flexible and adaptable
— Provide opportunities for seeing and touching
— Relate information to the visitor's prior experiences
— Find ways of making complex information simple
— Structure learning into small tasks

VISUAL IMPAIRMENT

Visual impairment is a sensory loss rather than a physical handicap. Persons with visual problems are classified according to the degree of sightedness that they possess. A person is considered legally blind if he has 20/200 visual acuity or less allowing him to see at 20 feet what a person with normal vision sees at 200 feet. The partially sighted are defined as having visual acuity between 20/70 and 20/200 in the better eye with maximum correction. Children able to use their visual sense to learn educational content are placed in a classroom for the visually sighted, while children able to learn only through their auditory and tactile senses are placed in a classroom structured for the visually impaired.

The visually impaired are dependent upon their functioning senses for much of their learning. They use their sense of touch, hearing, taste, and smell to familiarize themselves with their environment. Contrary to popular belief, a visually impaired person does not possess a sixth sense, rather he learns to use his remaining senses more effectively to interpret his environment. Having a visual problem does not affect a person's intellectual inherited capabilities. The person who becomes blind retains some *visual memory*, recollections of what he has seen prior to his blindness. However, in time the *memories* fade.

The visually impaired achieve much of their sense of space and their orientation through sound which provides location and distance cues. Of all the senses, touch is most similar to sight as both vision and touch are three dimensional sensory frames of reference. Through touch the visually impaired are highly verbal and dependent upon verbal descriptions for helping them to interpret their environment. Indeed the visually impaired learn about their surroundings through listening and touching. But while verbal descriptions are an integral part of their learning process, concrete experiences are equally important. The perception of light and color cannot be compensated by the other senses. Literacy for the visually impaired is achieved by the ability to read and write braille. The learning of braille, a system of writing using raised dots on paper, it is an abstract and structured process, and many children under the age of seven are unable to master it. Braille reading is slow, and *talking books,* long-playing phonographs, allow the blind to obtain information more quickly.

In the museum the visually impaired will usually need a docent, verbal description, and the opportunity to handle the objects they are learning about. The visually impaired must be able to experience in a concrete way if they are to come away with some conceptualization. The docent must couple the sensory experience with a verbal description and explanation. A detailed description of an object or process allows the visually impaired to conceptualize it in his mind. The docent should include in the description the texture, weight, shape, size, volume, and color of the item, keeping the descriptions concrete and related to things with which they are familiar. For example:

— The form of an Eskimo snow house can be compared to a ball cut in half.
— An object's size can be compared with the length of a bicycle, a school bus, or the child's height.
— Colors can be related to music, such as bright colors being associated with happy music.

If the docent is demonstrating a craft he should allow the children to place their hands on his hands as he demonstrates the method or technique.

The docent must be relaxed and enthusiastic throughout the guided visit. His language must be very descriptive and used as a teaching tool. The docent must remember that visually impaired people are not deaf and should not speak in a voice louder than his normal voice and should not hesitate to use words like *see* and *look* when talking.

HEARING IMPAIRED

Communication for a hearing impaired person is impeded by difficulties with either reception and/or expression of language. Deafness can affect internal as well as external speech. Language serves a social as well as a personal function in that one can engage in speech with others as well as speech with oneself. Other aspects of communication, speaking, comprehension, reading, and writing are also affected by hearing impairment. People having impaired hearing usually have well functioning speech mechanisms, but they must learn to use them properly. Cut off not only from sounds, but also speech, there are many social and learning opportunities in which the hearing impaired are unable to participate.

The hearing impaired receive information visually, either through lip reading or manual communication. In lip reading the person must learn that certain movements of the lips represent certain words. Lip reading is an attempt to help the hearing impaired person communicate more readily with the hearing world. Some sounds cannot be detected by watching a person's lips so that comprehension often is dependent not only upon reading lips but also upon the interpretation of facial expressions and gestures. Not all hearing impaired people know how to read lips, and indeed only 30 percent of the spoken language can be deciphered by most adept lip readers. Manual communication is a combination of sign language and finger spelling. In the manual alphabet, specific hand or finger symbols represent each letter, while in sign language, a single position of the fingers or movement of the hand may represent an entire phrase or expression. Language development for the hearing impaired remains several years below that of their peers, but inadequate language skills is not necessarily indicative of a low intelligence.

There are two categories of the hearing impaired: those born completely deaf or sustaining an early hearing loss that has prevented the learning of language and the hard of hearing who possess some hearing and need a hearing device to amplify sound. Having a hearing impairment can also mean that a person can hear high-pitched sounds but not low sounds or vice versa. A hearing aid cannot only make sounds louder but correct high or low pitch losses as well. Persons experiencing a 70 percent hearing loss are labeled as deaf while the hard of hearing experience a 30 percent loss. A person's hearing level or the lowest point at which he begins to hear sounds is measured in decibels. Decibels are measures of change in the intensity of sound and range from 1 to 130. Ordinary conversation measures from 50 to 60 decibels and 130 decibels registers so loud that it is painful. A person whose hearing loss is in the 20 to 60 decibel range is classified as hard of hearing, and a person unable to respond to sounds lower than 60 decibels is labeled as profoundly deaf. Children who are deaf before the age of three are not likely to retain normal speech and language patterns. The later a person loses his hearing, the more apt he is to retain normal speech patterns. The profoundly deaf express themselves in one or two words or by phrases. Their language is characterized by a limited vocabulary and different syntax.

People with impaired hearing need firsthand experiences with concrete items, thus learning activities should be organized around material that is manipulative. Demonstrations, books, and words are not nearly as effective for learning as hands-on activities. The docent should be standing in good light facing the group when communicating with the hearing impaired and use both gestures and facial expressions for communication. Language should be simple and free of abstractions. Information can be demonstrated, dramatized, or reflected in a picture or photograph. It is difficult for hearing impaired people to see an object and hear an explanation at the same time. So the docent needs to explain to the group about the object that they will be seeing and handling and give them lots of time to explore it.

MENTALLY HANDICAPPED

The mentally handicapped person needs a longer period of time to learn than the average person. There are three major classifications of mental retardation: the mildly retarded or educably mentally retarded (EMR), the trainable mentally retarded (TMR), and the profoundly mentally retarded (PMR). The educably mentally retarded (EMR) have an I. Q. between 70 and 75 and while having problems learning in a regular classroom, they can benefit to a degree from school. With proper training the EMR student is capable of reading and doing basic sixth grade school work. Eventually he may become a partially or totally self-supporting adult. An I. Q. between 30 and 50 characterizes the trainable mentally retarded (TMR). Although unable to learn reading, writing, and arithmetic they can acquire basic self-care routines, and adequate social habits and are capable as adults of

living in a sheltered workshop or institution. The custodial or profoundly mentally retarded person (PMR) has an I. Q. below 30 and is unable to be trained in self-care, socialization, or routine skills and requires help throughout life in order to survive. Some characteristics of the mentally retarded are —
— Limited reasoning ability
— Short attention span
— Limited power of association
— Greater comprehension of the concrete than the abstract
— Low frustration level

Special education programs adapt and modify the school curriculum to meet the individual needs of the mentally handicapped. The current educational trend is to integrate and include the mentally handicapped in as many activities with children of average intelligence as possible via the process called mainstreaming. Special classes in regular schools group children with the same exceptionality together to be taught by a specially trained teacher. The children, to the extent that their handicap allows, can participate in nonacademic areas with the rest of the school. Mainstreaming enables exceptional children to engage in academic work with other students in a regular classroom whenever possible. Residential schools provide children with a complete instructional program and a twenty-four hour, live-in situation. Some residential schools accept both day and residential students.

The docent must organize information and skills that he wishes to teach the mentally handicapped into small, simple steps that can be taught one at a time. He must provide explicit instructions and directions and limit the stimuli that the group receives. To learn there must be opportunities for the mentally handicapped to touch, to manipulate, and to experience the concrete. There must be continuous repetition, a movement from the general to the specific, from the concrete to the abstract, and from the egocentric to a broader perspective.

THE PHYSICALLY DISABLED

The physically disabled person is one who has an impairment that prevents normal movement and functioning. Wheelchairs, crutches, braces, and other aids are often needed to maximize movement. Persons having physical disabilities form a varied group who may or may not have normal intelligence. Cerebal palsy and muscular dystrophy are common physical handicaps. Cerebral palsy is a group of heterogeneous disabilities caused by brain damage that affects motor control. Muscular dystrophy is a hereditary disease characterized by the progressive deterioration of the muscles. With the disease the muscles become weak and eventually waste away. The physically disabled person may have —

— Jerky body movements
— A weak hand grasp
— Involuntary movement
— Sensory loss

Docents must remember that a wheelchair-seated person's eye level is a foot and a half below the eye level of the average standing person. This causes not only visual problems but also problems with hearing. Because the physically disabled person has problems turning his body or shifting positions, docents should make certain that the exhibit and/or object being discussed is in full view. The docent must also not automatically assume that the physically disabled person is mentally handicapped.

ADOLESCENTS

Adolescents are infrequent museum visitors and program participants. Museums have generally been ineffective in their efforts to serve the thirteen to nineteen-year-old age group. In many ways the habits and attitudes that characterize the teen make it difficult for the museum to satisfactorily serve them. The adolescent is intensely self-conscious and concerned with his peer group relationship. As a result any museum program that does not allow him to socialize with his friends is doomed to failure. Worried about his future, the adolescent pragmatically views the schooling process as preparation for adulthood. His school schedule is organized by subject disciplines with the adolescent spending a certain portion of his class day in the study of each discipline. This scheduling method makes it very difficult for these students to visit the museum during the school day since it means missing one or more of his academic classes. Hence museum programming for this audience has to be scheduled either after school or on weekends.

The traditional guided school visit doesn't meet the needs of the adolescent, and so the museum must explore some different kinds of programming for this audience. The museum should capitalize upon the adolescent's concern for the future by providing programs that stress vocational possibilities within the museum profession. Allowing the adolescent to work closely with a museum employee who serves as a mentor is another program possibility. Adolescent programming should emphasize the museum's role as a community resource and incorporate staff expertise and behind-the-scenes visits. There are no clearly defined guidelines for working successfully with this age group, rather the museum must experiment with various programming formats.

THE NONSCHOOL GROUP

Not all guided groups are school classes; many are youth groups, clubs, tourists, and families. If the docent is to structure a meaningful guided visit he must clearly understand the characteristics of the nonschool group. It is important that the docent remember that the purpose of the visit by a nonschool group is often more recreational than educational. The nonschool group is varied in interests, abilities, experiences, and sometimes even age. The group may range from the hobbyist or expert, possessing some special interest and expertise, to the novice. The visit may be seen as a sight-seeing excursion or an opportunity to experience the museum's major and most popular exhibits. Indeed the visit is often planned in response to the museum's publicity. Visitor expectations may be undefined, vague, and varied with the group being loosely organized and control relaxed. And most importantly, group members are chiefly concerned with having their individual expectations met.

The docent should encourage independent exploration of the exhibits, allowing sufficient amount of time for observing, including touching and other sensory experiences. The format should be fluid with numerous opportunities provided for questions from the visitors. The docents must learn from the group if there are any special exhibits that they wish to see and include those particular exhibits in the guided visit. The docent should elicit the group's help in organizing and focusing the time that they spend at the museum.

THE SPECIAL INTEREST GROUP

Special interest groups are homogeneous only in their area of special interest, for in all other ways they are exceedingly diverse. Educators, museum professionals, community organizations, and foreign visitors typify the special interest groups that visit the museum. The docent must ascertain the group's particular concerns and integrate them into the content of the guided visit. Often these groups are interested in knowing the museum's educational philosophy and history, budgetary and funding information, and staff size and qualifications. The groups should be given time to view the exhibits independently, ask questions, share information, concerns, and ideas with the docent, and interact with others in the group. There should also be activity-oriented experiences incorporated into the visit. The guided experiences should be relaxed, and its form should rely largely upon the group's responses.

CONCLUSION

The successful guided visit must evolve from the visitors. The docent must structure interpretative interactions that reflect the interests, abilities, and special needs of his audience. The traits of the visitors coupled with the information and concepts to be conveyed determine the interpretive techniques that the docent will use. Responsive reaction to the needs and characteristics of the group are essential if the guided visit is to be a meaningful learning experience for the group members involved.

Chapter 6

EVALUATING MUSEUM PROGRAMS

Education is what survives
when what has been learnt
has been forgotten
— B. F. Skinner, 1964

I N one way or another, this entire book can be related to
the notion of evaluation. Evaluation is an attempt to
interpret the results of your school tour program, your docent
education program, your museum program, etc. Evaluation is
part of the effort to reduce the number of decisions people make
that are based on unsupported evidence about what is happening.
Evaluation results may or may not support one's feelings about
what may or may not be happening. Evaluation data may shatter
one's favorite notion or dispel any illusion about what is happening as the result of a museum program. Some people reject all
attempts to evaluate. Part of that rejection probably has to do
with trust: Sometimes people are suspect with respect to the
evaluation process. They view evaluation results as either *good*
or *bad* instead of as a method for discovering program effectiveness for future planning considerations. It is important to remember that evaluation results in the collection of data. Data does
not judge; people do. Therefore, people must ensure that evaluation doesn't become a weapon to be used improperly. Thus,
any successful evaluation process must have its origin in an atmosphere of trust. Those museum persons in authority must
work to develop this atmosphere of trust by willing to be evaluated themselves and by serving as evaluation models.

In planning an evaluation program, you need to be certain that the devices you employ to collect the data you wish to collect do, in fact, collect the data that you intended to obtain. That means that you must know what kind of information your museum wants to collect and how you will collect this information. You should also know why you want to collect this information. For any information that you plan to collect, you should be able to answer two questions:

— What would our museum do with the data if we had it?
— Is the way that we plan to collect the data for the first question appropriate to my intention?

If you cannot supply acceptable answers to these two questions, then you probably should not take the time to collect that category of information.

WHY EVALUATE?

The main purpose of the museum evaluation program should be to ensure that the museum education program is meeting the needs of the museum visitors. Other purposes for evaluation include administrative decision making, program evaluation, personnel evaluation, and monetary (grant) purposes.

One example of evaluation or lack of evaluation can be found in programs supported by the National Endowment for the Arts (NEA). In 1980, using the peer review system, 600 panelists considered about 23,800 applications for NEA grants. In the category of painting, there were about 3,000 applications, each accompanied by slides of ten different works over which the six-person panel deliberated for five days of joint viewing and discussions. That works out to about a minute or less per application. As a result, the use of the peer review system has increasingly come under fire as an evaluation system. *It is generally accepted among artists that knowing a panelist greatly improves the odds of getting a grant. In a competitive, fast-moving process of elimination, intellectual aesthetic, and even personal cronyism is inevitably going to take precedence over the careful consideration of art, especially art that is off the beaten track, controversial, or perhaps just difficult to swallow at the first setting.* [1]

---

[1] Michael Ennis, "Untitled," *Texas Monthly, 11(8)*: 148 - 150, August, 1981.

People will evaluate museums including their personnel and programs either formally or informally. Informal evaluations may or may not include the aspects that should be emphasized as a schema for improving services in the future. Formal evaluations provide the means and methods needed to provide the accountability inherent in the justification for the use of public and private funds. It provides the basis for keeping the records needed to obtain future funding support, to respond to program modifications, and for evaluating the quality of museum programs. It appears that many museums are confusing quantity evaluations with quality, where the number of visitors who pass by an exhibit in thirty seconds is revered more than the quality of the exhibit they are passing by. Evaluation programs will certainly include — number of tours, number of docents, number of visitors, but evaluation should also emphasize the quality of the museum endeavor and whether or not the needs of its clientele are being met.

EVALUATING YOURSELF

Evaluation should begin with one's self, whether it be the beginning or experienced docent, or the museum administrator. Some self-evaluation questions for docents include the following:
Am I
— Prepared for the tour today?
— Ready to improve my next tour as a result of this tour?
— Showing interest in my tour group?
— A good listener?
— Responding to the needs of the visitors?
— Encouraging the visitors to use all their senses and not just sight?
— Trying to avoid using the word *no* on the tour?
— Interacting with other docents to obtain new ideas and to share ideas?
— Working cooperatively with the teacher if it is a school group?
— Establishing eye contact with the visitors?
— Having each of my tours evaluated in order to improve?
— Trying to develop a variety of methods?

— Learning to react objectively and with controlled emotions?
— Maintaining a positive attitude?
— Enthusiastic when working with a tour group?
— Developing the spirit of understanding and sympathy?
— Meeting the needs of my group?
— Including all members of my tour group in the discussions?
— Providing museum tours that are favorable to learning?

Do I

— Give directions with poise and assurance?
— Have a sufficient knowledge of the subject matter?
— Allow for individual differences?
— Praise when appropriate?
— Capitalize upon the best that any individual has to offer?
— Encourage visitor participation?
— View discipline on school tours as increasing ability in self-management rather than as mere repression by authority?
— Cope with interruptions resourcefully?
— Feel satisfied afterwards about the tour?
— Make sure that visitors enjoy my tour and want to return for another tour?
— Explain to my group what we will do and why before the tour begins?
— Communicate at the level of my group?
— Find out where my group is at before the tour begins?
— Change my approach to accommodate different groups?
— Know when to ask a question and when to make a statement?
— Suggest that visitors view exhibits from different levels, different angles, and different distances?
— Encourage visitors to observe differences as well as similarities among several exhibits?
— Give visitors time to observe and view exhibits on their own?
— Respond satisfactorily to the visitor that answers all my questions; to the visitor who purposely distracts others on the tour; to the quiet, shy visitor?
— React positively to evaluations of my tours?

EVALUATING THE DOCENT TRAINING PROGRAM

Many museums conduct a formal docent training program that is designed to prepare the docent for tours with a variety of groups, especially school groups. The training program may last anywhere from several hours to several months to a continuing program lasting throughout the tenure of the docent. Some training programs rely strictly upon informal evaluation to ascertain the effectiveness of a particular program. Unfortunately, these *value* judgments are not always either reliable or accurate when compared to the use of formal evaluations. Formal docent evaluations regarding docent performance should be submitted by not only the docent's supervisors, but also by the visitors that participate on the docents' tours. Most museum educators would agree that docents should know their subject matter, be able to accurately describe the artifacts and exhibits, and understand the major concepts relative to the purposes and organization of a particular gallery. However, it is equally important to also include the ability of the docent to apply that knowledge in the conduct of a tour. Thus, the docent training program should have the following components at the very least:

— Content background
— Exhibit instruction
— Communication skills, especially questioning
— Simulated tours
— Tour evaluation and analysis
— Practicing different tours
— Sequencing exhibits
— Pacing tours

It is important to note that the evaluation of docent background and tour performance is best accomplished as part of the entire program evaluation procedure that serves as a method for the continued improvement of museum programs.

One goal of the docent education program ought to be the development of a positive attitude towards museums and museum education. The Appendix includes a sample attitude assessment that we have used on a pre/post basis to determine attitudinal changes that occur as a result of the docent training program.

Also included in the Appendix is a sample docent profile that is an outgrowth of the assessment. Five of the sixty questions on the test relate to one of the twelve categories on the profile. Six categories (even numbers) on the profile are negative in nature. Six categories (odd numbers) on the profile are positive in nature. Strong agreement on the positive categories will result in a score of 15 for each category. Strong disagreement on the negative categories will result in a score of 15 for each category. Results of the pre/post assessment should be provided to all docents so that they know their entering attitude and how they have changed as a result of the training program. A scoring key may be obtained by writing on your museum stationery to: Dr. Gerald H. Krockover, Purdue University, Education Building, West Lafayette, Indiana 47907.

A less formal docent training evaluation could be developed that would use a number line rating scale, such as from one to five (lowest to highest). Sample questions might include the following:

— How would you rate the entire docent training program?
— How would you rate the general effectiveness of the lectures?
— How would you rate the overall effectiveness of the workshops?
— How would you rate the general organization of the training program?

Additional questions that may be asked include:

— If you have had prior experience as a docent, please indicate this as to type and duration.
— Which training sessions did you consider to be especially valuable and why? Which sessions were worthless and why?

Questions that could be asked after the new docents have completed several tours might include the following:

— Did the training adequately prepare you for giving tours? Why or why not?
— Did you enjoy the training program? Why or why not?
— How did you feel about the length of the training program?
— What suggestions do you have for improving the training program?

Evaluation of docents by a docent educator or experienced docent that exemplifies the type of tours that the museum is striving for can be accomplished in several ways. An evaluator can accompany the docent on several tours; the docent can submit audio tapes of tours for evaluation; or the docent can have several tours video taped for viewing at a later date. In every instance, the docent evaluator should meet personally with the docent being evaluated to discuss strong and weak points. However, emphasis should be placed upon the positive aspects, and docent evaluation should be a continuing feature, not a one time occurrence.

Sample questions that the docent evaluator may want to use include the following:

— Does the docent establish good rapport with the group?
— Does the docent present the material in a well-organized manner organized around a central concept or theme? Are the introduction, theme, clear transitions, and conclusion satisfactory?
— Does the docent give an effective presentation? Are the voice, mannerisms, vocabulary, logistics, and delivery satisfactory?
— Was the content of the presentation satisfactory?
— Are sufficient scope and depth, facts accurate, objects well chosen to illustrate theme, and appropriate visual elements used?
— Was the pace of the tour satisfactory? Did the docent demonstrate logical sequence, transition, anticipation of alternatives, and timing?
— Does the docent demonstrate an effective questioning technique? Were high level questions asked, good wait times shown, divergent questions asked, and visitor interaction encouraged?

Remember, if a docent scores low in any particular category, it may not be the fault of the docent, but rather the fault of the docent training program. Therefore, the docent training program must be continually modified to respond to docent concerns and perceived weaknesses in the program.

EVALUATING TOURS

Every museum visitor, whether on a guided or unguided tour, should be provided with the opportunity to evaluate the museum including its exhibits and programs. Younger visitors (preschool to third grade) can utilize a number line evaluation tied to matching faces ranging from a smile to a frown (*see* Figure 6-1 below).

DIRECTIONS: Place an X on the face that shows most

closely how you feel about each sentence.

1.   I like museums.

2.   Museums are fun.

3.   I like to go on tours.

4.   Museums are exciting.

Figure 6-1. Sample Evaluation Form
for Preschool and Primary Museum Visitors

Figure 6-1. (continued)

5. Museums are important.

6. Our guide was good.

7. Museums help me learn more about the world.

8. I wish we had more time for visiting museums.

9. Museums are a waste of time.

10. When I grow up, I want to work in a museum.

Older groups (fourth grade and up) can respond to their museum visit using a number line (1 to 5) response sheet, a yes - no checklist, or a question - response format. Sample evaluation questions for older groups might include the following:

— Rate the overall effectiveness of your tour (1 - low; 5 - high). Why did you give your tour this rating?
— Did you select to go on this tour yourself? Why or why not?
— Your tour was organized around a theme. Did you enjoy this type of theme tour? If not, what approach would you have preferred?
— Did our informational brochure help you understand what would happen when you arrived at the museum?
— Did your school class do any pretour activities to help prepare you for your museum visit? Why or why not?
— Did you enjoy the tour? Why or why not?
— What did you like most about the tour? Why?
— What did you like least about the tour? Why?
— Do you want to return to this museum for another visit? Why or why not?
— Did the tour meet your needs? Why or why not?
— State the best part of your tour.
— State the worst part of your tour.
— Complete these sentences.
Museums are. . .
The thing I like most about museums is. . .
The thing I like least about museums is. . .
I cannot understand why museums. . .
If I could change a museum, I would change. . .
If I could add something to a museum, I would add. . .
If I could run a museum, I would. . .
If I could tell about a museum, I would say. . .
— List all the things that you think a museum should contain to make it exciting. Which ones does this museum have? Which ones does this museum need?

To summarize, the main goal for evaluating museum programs is to ascertain the effectiveness of docent education programs, the ability of docents to provide tours that meet the needs of the visitors, and to assess the effects of those tours upon the visitors. Program evaluation is a continual, evolving process that has no end point. While our evaluation suggestions have focused upon the docent, all those who are a part of the museum team should be evaluated including the administrators and curatorial staff. Everyone who works in a museum should be evaluated in terms of effects upon visitors.

For example, questions such as those listed below should also be asked:

— Which exhibit is better and why?
— If you could change this exhibit, what would you change?
— Which method is most effective for docent training, Method X or Method Y?

The evaluation program should not focus exclusively upon the docent but rather upon the effectiveness of the programs that train the docent. All evaluating should be geared to making the most out of tours by emphasizing the use of objects and exhibits, generalizations, communicating with visitors, providing tours that meet the needs of visitors, and special entering and exit activities for visitors.

One sample entering (pretour) activity is shown in Figure 6-2. A sample exit activity is shown in Figure 6-3.

Evaluation can be ignored (in which case it will take place anyway); it can be informal; or it can be a formal part of the museum program. The choice is yours. Will you use evaluation as a learning experience or a weapon? Much in the way of evaluation presupposes that what is being presented is desired by the museum visitor. Wouldn't it be worthwhile to find out?

Directions: As you proceed through the museum, find a
               different exhibit that demonstrates each of
               these qualities. Plan to demonstrate this to
               the group upon completion of your tour.

    *Warmth can be seen in . . .

    *Silence can be felt in , . .

    *Quickness can be found in . . .

    *Funniness can be found in . . .

    *Beauty can be seen in . . .

    *Sorrow can be felt in . . .

    *Friendship can be seen in . . .

You can add five more below:

    *

    *

    *

    *

    *

Figure 6-2. Sample Entering Activity

Provide an <u>incomplete</u> guide book to each visitor at the end of the tour and have them <u>finish</u> the guide book by filling in the blanks.

Sample entries might include:

*An overview of the purpose of the museum.

*Exhibit highlights.

*Observations.

*Themes or general concepts.

*Space to invite additional questions to be discussed later.

*Suggestions for future exhibits and/or research.

*Space for general comments and impressions of the museum visit.

Figure 6-3. Sample Exit Activity

Appendix
WHAT IS YOUR ATTITUDE
TOWARDS MUSEUMS
AND MUSEUM EDUCATION

SAMPLE ASSESSMENT

THERE are some statements about museum education and museums in general on the next few pages. Some statements are about a person's feelings about the role of a docent. Some statements describe how docents should teach. You may agree with some of the statements and you may disagree with others. That is exactly what you are asked to do. By doing this, you will show your attitudes toward museum education and museums in general.

After you have carefully read a statement, decide whether you agree or disagree with it. If you agree, decide whether you agree mildly or strongly. If you disagree, decide whether you disagree mildly or strongly. Then find the space on the answer sheet that agrees with your feelings and blacken it in.

A. . . If you agree strongly
B. . . If you agree mildly
C. . . If you disagree mildly
D. . . If you disagree strongly

Adapted from *What is Your Attitude Towards Science and Science Teaching*, Marvin H. Bratt, Unpublished Ph.D. Thesis, Purdue University, West Lafayette, Indiana, 1974.

Example:
00. I would like to make lots of money.

A	B	C	D
██			

(The person who marked this example agrees strongly that he would like to make lots of money.)

1. One fact elementary children should learn is that the air is approximately 20 percent oxygen.
2. Docents should plan and evaluate museum tours.
3. Most children should be able to interpret a graph — at least by sixth grade.
4. Visitors should design their own museum projects.
5. The role of the docent is to present concepts for the visitors to learn.
6. A docent should be a resource person rather than an information giver.
7. I should learn as much as the visitors when I conduct a tour.
8. I do not understand museum education, and I do not want to learn about it.
9. The visitors should progress through the museum in the sequence that I set up.
10. The docent should tell the visitors what they have to learn and know.
11. It should be more important to establish a personal relationship with visitors than to worry about the subject matter I transmit.
12. In giving tours, a docent might spend more time listening to the visitors than talking to them.
13. Visitors should not evaluate their own museum projects.
14. The docent should help the visitor find ways to attain his goals, but not set them up for him.
15. Process skills, such as observing, thinking, measuring, are very important things to be developed, especially in the elementary grades.
16. The docent should have top priority in decision making over visitors.

17. The docent should respond to the visitor rather than the visitor responding to the docent.
18. Visitors need to know the basic facts in a museum before they can understand the concepts.
19. Visitors must learn certain facts in museums so that they can do well in later life.
20. Visitors should feel that they can sit and discuss any subject at any time with a docent.
21. I understand museums and I want to lead tours.
22. Docents should be solely responsible for assigning visitors to tours.
23. In museum education visitors must be told what they are to learn.
24. Visitors can and should learn to evaluate themselves; docents should help visitors do this.
25. The docent should teach the basic skills such as observing, measuring, and classifying.
26. Docents should teach their specialities.
27. Visitors and docents should both be free to express their views in the museum.
28. The needs of visitors are irrelevant to museum education; visitors don't know what they should know.
29. As visitors experiment, the docent should ask leading questions.
30. Museums are pretty easy to understand.
31. Visitors should feel that they may discuss their personal goals in a subject matter area with any docent.
32. Process skills (observing, classifying, inferring, etc.) are the most important things to be developed by visitors through museums.
33. The docent should assign museum projects to visitors.
34. I like museums, and I probably am/will be a better docent than most other docents.
35. Visitors learn best to make decisions when they are given the opportunity to make decisions.
36. I am afraid to be a docent because I don't understand museums myself.
37. The docent should be accountable for a visitor's knowledge.

38. I just never will understand museum education.
39. Visitors and docents should both respect the knowledge, resourcefulness, and creativity of each other.
40. A docent should teach the basic facts of museums.
41. Docents should cover specific areas for each grade level on a tour.
42. The idea of museum education scares me.
43. Docents should tell visitors about museum projects.
44. Visitors should feel that what they have to say in museums is just as important as what the docents have to say.
45. Visitors should not plan their own museum projects.
46. If a project does not come out right, the docent should tell the visitor the answer so they will not be lost.
47. Visitors should learn to evaluate their own museum projects.
48. It is a docent's responsibility to tell visitors which things are important about museums.
49. I do/will not teach very much about museums.
50. Elementary children should learn how to conduct an experiment.
51. I feel I am very well prepared for museum education.
52. The docent should arrange things so that visitors spend more time experimenting than listening at the museum.
53. Visitors cannot learn unless they pay attention to what the docent has to say.
54. I think I understand the work of museums.
55. A fact children should know is that blood carries oxygen to the cells — at least by the sixth grade.
56. Visitors should discover for themselves that learning is their responsibility; docents should help visitors learn how to learn.
57. Docents should help visitors identify problems.
58. Docents should not have to be concerned with visitor's problems.
59. It is important for children to know why iron rusts — at least by the sixth grade.
60. Docents should teach the visitors, not the facts of the museums.

PROFILE OF YOUR ATTITUDE TOWARDS MUSEUMS
AND MUSEUM EDUCATION

SAMPLE PROFILE

NAME_____ POSTTEST DATE_____

PRETEST DATE_____

	Points	Pretest Score	Posttest Score	Change (+) or (-)
1. The idea of museum education is attractive to me.	15	____	____	____
2. I do not like the thought of museum education.	15	____	____	____
3. There are certain museum skills that visitors should know.	15	____	____	____
4. There are certain museum facts that visitors should know.	15	____	____	____
5. Museum education should be guiding or facilitating of learning. The docent becomes a resource person.	15	____	____	____
6. Museum education should be a matter of telling visitors what they are to learn.	15	____	____	____
7. In museums and museum education, the needs of visitors and docents should be more important than the subject matter.	15	____	____	____
8. In museums and museum education, covering subject matter should be more important than the needs of visitors.	15	____	____	____

	Points	Pretest Score	Posttest Score	Change (+) or (-)
9. Educational programs should find docents and visitors working together for mutual benefit so they both learn something.	15	_____	_____	_____
10. The docent should be the authority in the museum. He/she ought to be there to teach and the visitors should be there to learn from him/her.	15	_____	_____	_____
11. Visitors and docents alike are responsible for learning that takes place in a museum. Visitors should have as much to say about their learning activities and their evaluation as docents.	15	_____	_____	_____
12. The docent should be the sole determiner of the activities. It is he/she that should plan and evaluate each tour.	15	_____	_____	_____
TOTAL...............	180	_____	_____	_____

BIBLIOGRAPHY

Adams, Barbara: *Like It Is: Facts and Feelings About Handicaps From Kids Who Know.* New York, Walker, 1979.

Agency for Instructional Television: *Think About Television Series.* Box A, Bloomington, Indiana.

Alexander, Edward P.: *Museums in Motion.* Nashville, American Association for State and Local History, 1979.

American Association for Gifted Children: *On Being Gifted.* New York, Walker, 1978.

American Association for State and Local History Technical Leaflet 73: Exhibit Planning: Ordering Your Artifacts Interpretively. *History News, 29 (4),* April 1979.

American Association for State and Local History Technical Leaflet 91: Designing Your Exhibit: Seven Ways to Look at an Artifact. *History News, 31 (11),* November 1976.

American Association for State and Local History Technical Leaflet 105: Historic Houses As Learning Laboratories: Seven Teaching Strategies. *History News, 33 (4),* April 1978.

American Association for State and Local History Technical Leaflet 106: Financing Your History Organization: Setting Goals. *History News, 33 (7),* July 1978.

American Association for State and Local History Technical Leaflet 113: Authentic Costuming for Historic Site Guides. *History News, 34 (3),* March 1979.

American Association for State and Local History Technical Leaflet 124: Working Effectively With the Press: A Guide for Historical Societies. *History News, 35 (2),* February 1980.

American Association of Museums: In Robbins, Michael (Ed.): *America's Museums: The Belmont Report.* Washington, D. C., 1969.

American Association of Museums: *Museums: Their New Audience.* Washington, D. C., 1972.

Andrews, Dathryne, and Asia, Cardi: Teenagers' Attitudes About Art Museums. *Curator, 22 (3):* 224-232, September 1979.

Art to Zoo: *News from Schools from the Smithsonian Institution.* Washington, D. C., Publication of the Office of Elementary and Secondary Education.

Banks, James A., and Clegg, Ambrose A., Jr.: *Teaching Strategies for the Social Studies: Inquiry, Valuing, and Decision Making.* Reading, Massachusetts, Addison-Wesley, 1973.

Barbe, Walter: *The Exceptional Child.* Washington, Center for Applied Research, 1973.

Bigge, Morris: *Learning Theories for Teachers.* New York, Harper and Row, 1976.

Biological Sciences Curriculum Study: *Energy and Society: Investigations in Decision Making.* Northbrook, Illinois, Hubbard Scientific, 1979.

Bloom, Benjamin: *Taxonomy of Educational Objectives: The Cognitive Domain.* New York, David McKay, 1956.

Borun, Minda: *Exhibit Evaluation: An Introduction.* In Draper, Linda (Ed.): *The Visitor and the Museum.* Berkeley, Lowie Museum of Anthropology.

Borun, Minda: *Measuring the Immeasurable: A Pilot Study of Museum Effectiveness.* Washington, D. C., Association of Science-Technology Centers, 1977.

Boulanger, David, and Smith, John: *Educational Principles and Techniques.* Portland, United States Department of Agriculture, Forest Service General Technical Report, 1973.

Bowley, Agatha, and Gardner, Leslie: *The Handicapped Child.* London, Churchill Livingstone, 1972.

Bradshaw, Mary: A pragmatic Approach to Museum Interpretation. American Association for State and Local History Technical Leaflet 65, *History News, 28 (8),* August 1973.

Bridge, R. Gary: Cultural Vouchers. *Museum News,* pp. 21-26, March/April 1976.

Brown, George I.: *Human Teaching for Human Learning.* New York, Viking Press, 1971.

Bunning, Richard: A Perspective on the Museum's Role in Community Adult Education. *Curator, 17 (1):* 56-63, March 1974.

Burcow, G. Ellis: *Introduction to Museum Work.* Nashville, The American Association for State and Local History, 1975.

Caplan, Frank, and Caplan, Theresa: *The Power of Play.* Garden City, Anchor Press, 1973.

Carin, Arthur A., and Fund, Robert B.: *Developing Questioning Techniques: A Self-Concept Approach.* Columbus, Charles E. Merrill Publishing, 1971.

Carner, Richard L.: Levels of Questioning. *Education, 83:* 546-550, Mary 1963.

Cobb, Vicki: *How to Really Fool Yourself.* New York, J. B. Lippincott, 1981.

Cobb, Vicki: *Lots of Rot.* New York, Lippincott Junior Books, 1981.

Cobb, Vicki: *Science Experiments You Can Eat.* New York, Lippincott Junior Books, 1972.

Collins, Zipporah W.: *Museums, Adults, and the Humanities: A Guide to Educational Programming.* Washington, D. C., American Association of Museums, 1981.

Coon, Herbert, and Alexander, Michelle: *Energy Activities for the Classroom.* Columbus, ERIC/SMEAC Information Reference Center, 1976.

Copeland, Mrs. Lammot du Pont: The Role of Trustees: Selection and Responsibilities. American Association for State and Local History Technical Leaflet 72, *History News, 29 (3),* March 1974.

Council on Museums and Education in the Visual Arts: *The Art Museum as Educator.* Berkeley, University of California Press, 1978.

Cowen, Philip: *Piaget: With Feeling.* New York, Holt, Rinehart and Winston, 1978.

Curator Magazine, New York Quarterly Publication of the American Museum of Natural Science.

DeVito, Alfred, and Krockover, Gerald H.: *Activities Handbook for Energy Education.* Santa Monica, Scott Foresman, Good Year Books, 1981.

DeVito, Alfred, and Krockover, Gerald H.: *Creative Sciencing: A Practical Approach.* 2nd ed., Boston, Little, Brown and Company, 1980.

DeVito Alfred, and Krockover, Gerald H.: *Creative Sciencing: Ideas and Activities for Teachers and Children,* 2nd ed. Boston, Little, Brown and Company, 1980.

Dickinson, Rita: *Caring for the Gifted.* North Quincy, Massachusetts, Christopher, Publishing Company, 1970.

Docents on Town, Washington D. C., Office of Museum Programs, Smithsonian Institution, 2235 Arts and Industries, 1979.

Dodd, N., and Hickson, W. (Eds): *Drama and Theatre in Education.* London, Heinemann Educational Books, 1979.

Early Adolescence: Perspectives and Recommendations. Washington, D. C., National Science Foundation, 1978.

Early American Life, Early American Society, P. O. Box 1831, Harrisburg, Pennsylvania.

Eble, Kenneth E.: *The Craft of Teaching.* San Francisco, Jossey-Bass, 1976.

Fraenkel, Jack: Ask the Right Questions, *Clearinghouse, 41:* 199-203, December 1966.

Fraenkel, Jack R.: *Helping Students Think and Value: Strategies for Teaching the Social Studies.* Englewood Cliffs, New Jersey, Prentice-Hall, 1973.

Gagne, Robert: The Acquisition of Knowledge. In Wittrock, M. C. (Ed.): *Learning and Instruction.* Berkeley, McCutcheon Publishing, 349-362, 1977.

Games Magazine, P. O. Box 10145, Des Moines, Iowa 50340.

Gardner, John: How to Prevent Organizational Dry Rot. *Harper's Magazine, 21,* October 1965.

Gardner, Martin: Aha. *Scientific American,* San Francisco, W. H. Freeman, 1978.

Gearheart, Bill R., and Weishahn, Mel W.: *The Handicapped Student In The Regular Classroom.* St. Louis, C. V. Mosby Company, 1980.

George, Gerald: Why Applications Fail. *Humanities, 21,* January-February 1980.

Gifted Children Newsletter, 530 University Avenue, Palo Alto, California.

Greenes, Carole, and Seymour, Dale: *Successful Problem Solving Techniques.* Palo Alto, Creative Publications, 1978.

Gross, Ronald: *The Lifelong Learner: A Guide to Self-Development.* New York, Simon and Schuster, 1977.

Grove, Richard: Pioneers in American Museums: John Cotton Dana. *Museum News,* pp. 32-39, May-June 1978.

Handford, Robert T. E.: *The Complete Book of Puppets and Puppeteering.* New York, Drake Publishers, 1976.

Hechinger, Nancy: Seeing Without Eyes. *Science 81, 2, 2:* 38-43, March 1981.

Hiemstra, Roger: *Guiding the Older Adult Learner.* Columbus, ERIC Clearinghouse on Adult, Career, and Vocational Education, 1980.

Holt, John C.: *How Children Fail.* New York, Dell Publishing, 1971.

Houch, Oliver A.: *The Present of All.* Washington, D. C., National Wildlife Federation, 1974.

Hunkins, Francis, P.: Using Questions to Foster Pupils' Thinking. *Education, 87:* 82-87, October 1966.

Hymes, James L.: *Teaching the Child Under Six.* Columbus, Charles Merrill Publishing Company, 1968.

Inglis, Ruth Langdon: *A Time to Learn.* New York, Dial City Press, 1973.

Instructor, 757 Third Avenue, New York.

Judson, Horace Freeland: *The Search for Solutions.* New York, Holt, Rinehart and Winston, 1980.

Kamien, Janet: *What If You Couldn't. . .?* New York, Charles Scribner's Sons, 1979.

Kenney, Alice: Museums from a Wheelchair. *Museum News, 53, 4:*14-17, November-December 1974.

Klebaner, Ruth: Questions That Teach. *Teacher, 81 (10):*76-77, March 1964.

Krieger, Terry, and Parks, Timothy: NEH Learning Museums. *Museum News,* pp. 25-28, May-June 1978.

Krockover, Gerald H.: Dialing Down the Energy Crisis. *Science and Children, 13, 2:*18-20, October 1975.

Krockover, Gerald H.: The Energy Book. New York, *Instructor,* 1978.

Krockover, Gerald H., and Hauck, Jeanette: Training for Docents: How To Talk to Visitors. American Association for State and Local History Technical Leaflet 125, *History News, 35 (3)*, March 1980.

Larrabee, Eric (Ed.): *Museums and Education*. Washington, D. C., Smithsonian Institution Press, 1968.

Learning: The Magazine for Creative Teaching Education Today, 530 University Avenue, Palo Alto, California.

Lobel, Arnold: *Fables*. New York, Harper Junior Books, 1981.

Low, Shirley P.: Historic Site Interpretation: The Human Approach. American Association for State and Local History Technical Leaflet 32, *History News, 20 (11)*, November 1965.

Lowery, Lawrence F. (Ed.): *Learning About Learning*. Berkeley, University of California, School of Education, 1973.

Lowery, Lawrence F: *A Person Training Program for Docents*. Oakland, Oakland Museum Association, 1976.

Lynch, William: *Are You Ready for the Handicapped?* Bloomington, Indiana University, School of Education, 1978.

Machlis, Gary, and McDonough, Maureen: *Children's Interpretation: A Discovery Book for Interpreters*. National Park Service, Seattle, University of Washington's College of Forest Resources, 1978.

McLanathan, Richard: Museums and the Future: United We Stand. *Museum News, 6,* January-February 1978.

Museum Magazine, 260 Madison Avenue, New York.

Museum News, Journal of the American Association of Museums, 1055 Thomas Jefferson Street, N. W., Washington, D. C.

National Center for Educational Statistics: 1979 Program Survey. U. S. Department of Education, 1980.

National Endowment for the Humanities, Division of Public Programs: *Guidelines, Museums and Historical Organizations*. Washington, D. C., 1979.

National Geographic, Journal of the National Geographic Society, 17th and M Streets, N. W., Washington, D. C.

National History, American Museum of Natural History, Central Park West of 79th Street, New York.

Newsom, Barbara, and Silver, Adele Z. (Eds.): *The Art Museum as Educator*. Berkeley, University of California Press, 1977.

Newton, E. S.: Andragogy: Understanding the Adult as a Learner. *Journal of Reading,* pp. 361-363, February 1977.

Peachnent, B.: *Educational Drama*. London, MacDonald and Evans, Ltd., 1976.

Piaget, Jean: *The Essential Piaget*. New York, Basic Books, 1977.

Postman, Neil: *Teaching as a Conserving Activity*. New York, Delacorte Press, 1979.

Postman, Neil and Weingartner, Charles: *Teaching as a Subversive Activity*. New York, Dell Publishing, 1969.

Project GAP (Gifted Academic Program), Concept Curriculum for the Gifted (K-8): *Problem Solving, Change, Reasoning, Signs and Symbols*. Matteson, Illinois, Matteson School District Number 162, 1981.

Reibel, Daniel: The Use of Volunteers in Museums and Historical Societies. *Curator, 17 (1)*: 16-26, March 1974.

Ripley, Dillon: *The Sacred Grove: Essays on Museums.* Washington, D. C., Smithsonian Institution Press, 1969.

Robers, Carl: *On Becoming A Person.* Boston, Houghton Mifflin, 1961.

Roucek, Joseph: *The Slow Learner.* New York, Philosophical Library, 1969.

Royal Ontario Museum: *Communicating With the Museum Visitor: Guidelines for Planning.* Toronto, Royal Ontario Museum, 1976.

Rubik's Cube. New York, Ideal Toy, 1981.

Sanderlin, Owenita: *Teaching Gifted Children.* New York, A. S. Barnes, 1973.

Saunders, Norris M.: *Classroom Questions: What Kinds?* New York, Harper and Row, 1966.

Schioeder, Fred E. H.: *Seven Ways to Look at an Artifact.* American Association for State and Local History Technical Leaflet 91, 1977.

Science and Children, National Science Teachers Association, 1742 Connecticut Avenue, N. W., Washington, D. C.

Science 82, American Association for the Advancement of Science, 1515 Massachusetts Avenue, N. W., Washington, D. C.

Screven, Chandler G.: A Bibliography on Visitor Education Research. *Museum News, 56,* March-April 1979.

Screven, Chandler G.: *The Measurement and Facilitation of Learning in the Museum Environment: An Experimental Analysis.* Washington, D. C., Smithsonian Institution Press, 1974.

Slides with a Purpose. Eastman Kodak Company, Dept 412-L, Rochester, New York.

Smith, Patricia: Against Segregating the Blind. *Museum News, 55, 3*: 10-11, January-February 1977.

Smithsonian Institution, 900 Jefferson Drive, Washington, D. C.

Sneider, Cary I., Eason, Laurie P., and Friedman, Alan J.: Summative Evaluation of a Participatory Science Exhibit. *Science Education, 63*: 25-36, 1979.

Spolin, Viola: *Improvisational Theater.* Evanston, Northwestern University Press, 1970.

Spolin, Viola: *Theater Game File.* St. Louis, Cenbrel, 1975.

Strasser, Ben B.: Posing Productive Questions. *Science and Children, 4*: 9-10, April 1967.

Striker, Susan: *The Anti-Coloring Book of Exploring Space on Earth.* New York, Holt, Rinehart and Winston, 1980.

Striker, Susan: *The Fourth Anti-Coloring Book.* New York, Holt, Rinehart and Winston, 1981.

Swinney, H. J. (Ed.): *Professional Standards for Museum Accreditation.* Washington, D. C., American Association of Museums, 1978.

Tilden, Freeman: *Interpreting Our Heritage,* 6th ed., Chapel Hill, University of North Carolina Press, 1974.

Toffler, Alvin: *Future Shock*. New York, Random House, 1970. Studies in Education, 1967.

Tough, Allen: *Learning Without a Teacher*. Toronto, Ontario Institute for Studies in Education, 1967.

Tough, Allen: Major Learning Efforts: Recent Research and Future Directions. *Adult Education, 28*: 250-263, 1978.

UNESCO: Museums and Children Issue. Quarterly Review, 31 (3), 1979.

UNESCO: Museums Imagination and Education. Switzerland, Arts Graphiques Coop Suisse, 1973.

UNESCO: The Organization of Museums — Practical Advice. Paris, Imprimerie Union, 1960.

U. S. Department of Energy: *Award Winning Energy Education Activities for Elementary and High School Teachers*. Oak Ridge, Tennessee, 1980.

Vail, Priscilla: *The World of the Gifted Child*. New York, Walker, 1979.

Vanderway, Richard: Planning Museum Tours. American Association for State and Local History Technical Leaflet 93, *History News*, 32 (3), March 1977.

Verdium, John R. et. al.: *Adults Teaching Adults*. Austin, Learning Concepts, 1977.

Wagner, B. J.: *Dorothy Heathcote: Drama as a Learning Medium*. Washington, D. C., National Education Association, 1976.

Wagner, Richard: *Famous Flying Machines to Color Cutout and Fly*. Los Angeles, Price, Stern, Sloan Publishers, 1981.

Way, Brian: *Development Through Drama*. New York, Longman, 1979.

Weitzman, David: *My Backyard History Book*. Boston, Little, Brown, 1975.

Wheeler, Robert: Effective Public Relations: Communicating Your Image. American Association for State and Local History Technical Leaflet 3, *History News, 28 (3)*, March 1973.

William, Patterson: Find Out Who Donny Is. *Museum News, VII*, 7: 42-45, April 1974.

Wittlin, Alma: *Museums: In Search of a Usable Future*. Cambridge, MIT Press, 1970.

Zetterberg, Hans: *Museums and Adult Education*. Great Britain, International Council of Museums, 1968.

Zetterberg, Hans L.: In Kelly, Augustus M. (Ed.): *Museums and Adult Education*. Fairfield, New Jersey, 1969.

INDEX

147